I0820201

BACKYARD CUTTING GARDEN

Small-Space Blooms to Grow, Harvest, and Arrange in Every Season

Trisha Snyder

SCHIFFER CRAFT

4880 Lower Valley Road • Atglen, PA 19310

Other Schiffer Craft Books on Related Subjects:

Sow, Grow, and Harvest: A Year-Round Guide to Gardening and Arranging Cut Flowers, Chantal Remmert, ISBN 978-0-7643-6898-1

Starting Your Floral Design Studio: A Creative Guide to Finding Your Style, Growing Your Business, and Nurturing Your Dream, Justine Beaussart, ISBN 978-0-7643-6939-1

Framing Floral Techniques: Floral Design Skill Building, Inspirations & Explorations, Renee Tucci, ISBN 978-0-7643-6200-2

Library of Congress Control Number: 2025939812

Designed by Lori Malkin Ehrlich
Front cover design by Lindsay Hess
Photography by Angelique Jasmin Photography
Edited by Kaylee Schofield
Type set in Brandon Grotesque, Quinn Text, Adventures Unlimited Script

ISBN: 978-0-7643-7132-5
ePub: 978-1-5073-0641-3
Printed in China

10 9 8 7 6 5 4 3 2 1

Published by Schiffer Craft
An imprint of Schiffer Publishing, Ltd.
4880 Lower Valley Road
Atglen, PA 19310
Phone: (610) 593-1777; Fax: (610) 593-2002
Email: Info@schifferbooks.com
Web: www.schifferbooks.com

To my mom.

*You not only exemplified how
to nurture flowers and create a
beautiful garden, but you (and dad)
also nurtured and loved me, and
gave me a secure and loving home
in which I could flourish.*

CONTENTS

PART THREE: THE PROJECTS • 132

WELCOME

Imagine: It's a beautiful summer morning. The sun is just coming up and there is a bit of mist over the fields. You, dressed in your cutest summer outfit, take your bucket, clippers, and inspiration to your boundless cutting garden, filled with blooms (and no weeds, of course!) just waiting for you to come and get them! After you cut, you head inside to arrange your blooms just as you had envisioned. Ah! It's all so perfect.

Wait a minute!

Let's be realistic. It's not that simple, and that, I believe, is why most people have never tackled this seemingly daunting task. Or maybe they know from experience that it's not going to be that idyllic.

When I was a young, married woman, I had these same desires. Even though I grew up surrounded by my mom's beautiful flower beds, I knew virtually nothing about cut flowers, except that zinnias fit into that category.

What got me hooked was having a property of my own that already had a few established cutting flowers. Peonies, roses, irises. I still remember that first vase of flowers I put together from the flowers blooming outside my door. I truly thought there was nothing more beautiful than that arrangement. I was officially intrigued!

You may have tried to grow cutting flowers before, but in the end, something discouraged you. Maybe it was bugs,

disease, drought, or simply having no idea what or when to plant. Even though you would like to have a cutting garden of your own, you either don't know where to start, what to grow, or if it's even possible with the small amount of space that you have.

Being in the cut-flower business for over 24 years now, I've talked to many aspiring gardeners who would like to have a cutting plot but are longing for a more realistic, manageable, homeowner-sized garden. Everyday people who just want to grow a small patch of cut flowers they can utilize and enjoy, people who are overwhelmed by the thought of a huge cutting garden, or even aspiring entrepreneurs who want to start their own flower business all have this question in common: "What are easy, reliable cut flowers I can grow in a small space and see blooming continually throughout the growing season?" If you resonate with that question, you've opened the right book.

Of all the existing books on flower gardening, I haven't yet seen one that details how to grow a cutting garden in a small space. Most people don't have an acre or two to play with and certainly don't have the time to maintain a large garden, but they still want the experience and joy of growing and cutting their own flowers. They just want it to be a manageable plot that won't take a lot of time and skill to maintain. A space they can transition to from the indoors and be transported to a paradise of seasonal flowers. They want some instruction and inspiration on how to use these flowers and create beautiful arrangements with them.

That's what this book is about. I hope to give you a starting point, a hopeful and practical plan for how to make this a reality in your own backyard. I will introduce a specific plan for what exactly to plant, a schedule of what to do and when, and types and descriptions of flowers to grow. There are plenty of ideas for how to arrange your flowers in almost every season of the year. Of course, you can change things around to fit your specific space or preferences. I just hope to inspire you to start so that you can experience the joy of your own backyard cutting garden!

OPPOSITE: Our cutting garden, bursting with blooms.

LEFT: Fresh-picked daffodils.

BOTTOM: There's nothing like picking flowers you've grown yourself.

THE FLOURISH STORY

Flourish had its humble beginnings as a small cut-your-own garden in our front yard beside the busy road that we live on. When I told my husband that I would like to plant a cutting garden, he graciously agreed, although I'm sure he had no idea of what he was ultimately saying yes to. Neither did I, for that matter! So, out went the perfect lawn, and in went my dream garden: a small 15-by-15-foot area composed entirely of cutting flowers. A new business start-up, yes, but also a place for me to unabashedly cut whatever flowers were blooming and bring them into my house to enjoy. It was a dream come true. An unexpected passion rekindled inside me from years before.

My love of flowers and growing things came to life slowly throughout my childhood. My mom and grandmother were both amazing gardeners and had more than your average homeowner's share of flower beds and landscaping. One of my earliest memories is walking around my grandmother's property with my aunts and mom on the "garden tour." Every time we were there for a family meal during the growing season, we would walk through her property to see what was blooming. I remember the ladies fawning over her hyacinths, peonies, and dahlias. She delighted in having others enjoy her colorful gardens, and there was much to see and appreciate.

My mom was constantly out in her gardens, making new beds, edging the existing ones, weeding, mulching, and planting trees. (She would say, "The best time to plant a tree is three years ago," meaning you'll never regret planting a tree sooner rather than later!). She transformed the grounds around our farmhouse (where my dad was born in 1939) into a lush landscape with deep flower beds, many trees, and lots of natural beauty.

So, when the time came for my husband and me to move into our own

LEFT: My mom in the garden, circa 1980.

BOTTOM: The family farmhouse, with its lush gardens.

little farmhouse with a bit of land, I realized that this love of the outdoors and heritage of gardening had been growing in me all along but was now burgeoning. Suddenly I was on fire with the urge to plant flower beds of my own. I found myself doing all the things I remembered my mom doing. It came so naturally and brought me such joy. My favorite days were the ones where I found myself covered in dirt, grass stains, and the fresh smell of the earth. And those are still my favorite days!

I vividly remember the first bouquet I cut from our property. The irises, peonies, and roses were blooming in my flower bed, so I cut them, arranged them very simply in a vase, and put them on the coffee table. I thought that I had died and gone to heaven—the simplicity of those flowers was beautiful to me, and I was so proud that it all came from my yard. I was officially hooked.

What could be better than having beautiful flowers growing in your backyard and then bringing them inside to beautify the house? I started looking at the landscape around my property in a completely different way. On my trips to the greenhouse and nursery, I would look at all the options with new eyes. "Can I cut that? Does it have a nice long stem? Will it last in water? Does that bush give a branch full of flowers? Would that be good foliage for an arrangement? When does it flower?" Cutting material became my new passion and the standard for all my new plant purchases!

In 2001, our cut-flower business officially began.

I began to think that maybe I could grow flowers and sell them by the roadside, but my challenge as a young grower was, "How do I even know what to grow?" I knew the basics, but a book like this to show me the step-by-step process of how to get started would have been incredibly helpful. How do I know what to plant so that I have flowers throughout the whole growing season? What are the best varieties to grow? How do I grow them?

My favorite days were the ones where I found myself covered in dirt, grass stains, and the fresh smell of the earth.

I decided to start with my first flower obsession: tulips. In the fall of 2000, a friend and I planted about 100 tulips and put them to bed for the long, cold winter. Imagine my excitement the following spring as the tips of the first tulips appeared through the thawing soil, developing into long-stemmed, gorgeous buds! My dream of a cut-flower business, although very small, was officially a reality.

After I had been in business for a year or two, a few women I knew from church asked me to do their wedding flower arrangements. I agreed because they knew I was just getting started with floral design, and their expectations (and budgets) were very low. It was a great way for me to get my foot in the door. As word got out and more and more people started asking me to do their flower arrangements, I realized I needed some real floral education!

After hearing about Longwood Gardens' Continuing Education Program (in Kennett Square, Pennsylvania), I took my very first floral design class. Never had learning been so fun or exciting! This was exactly what I needed. I remember massaging my pained face on the drive home because I had been smiling for the entire eight hours of class. Over the next few years, I completed enough classes and the final exam to receive my Floral Design Certificate from Longwood. I enjoyed every moment of those classes. This is also where the dream of hosting our own classes at Flourish was born. If I was having this much fun learning about flowers, then I was sure that other people in my own community would too.

Fast-forward to today: We now host over 30 flower-centric classes and on-site events every year, average more than 80 weddings a year, and supply our community with flowers when they call in or order on our website. I could have never imagined all this when I was planting that little 15-by-15-foot garden back in 2000, but the garden is still at the heart of my business, and I love to see the beauty it produces year after year.

Through the years I have learned that some flowers are easier to grow and some

ABOVE: We've grown since that first bed of tulips!

LEFT: Flourish is now a hub for flower lovers near and far.

...the garden is still at the heart of my business and I love to see the beauty it produces year after year.

are harder. Honestly, some are not worth our time, while some are superstars that we can't do without. In this book, I hope to give you that golden list of winners—easy-to-grow and hardworking cut flowers to have in your garden that have earned their place in ours. Of course, you can always change out any flowers listed in this book that are not your favorites, but let's explore together and get you on the road to your own flower hopes and dreams.

BELOW: Preparing flowers for weekly subscription customers.

PART ONE

GETTING STARTED

Like many things in life, flower gardening projects will be more successful if you follow a plan. Choosing your plot location and garden layout will take some consideration; once you have started, it's not so easy to undo a garden plot. So, let's consider the best spot for your garden.

To choose a site for your garden, take a walk around your property with a tape measure in hand. To utilize the garden plan in this book, you will want to choose a 12-by-12-foot site that gets at least six to eight hours of sun a day. You can certainly go smaller or bigger or use a different configuration than a square. Just modify the plan to make it work for you. It may be best to pick out a potential spot and keep an eye on it throughout the day to make sure that it gets enough sun. Just keep in mind that the angle of the sun, as well as the duration of light in winter, is quite different than in summer.

GARDEN LAYOUT

LOCATION IS EVERYTHING

As strange as it sounds, you will most likely want to tuck away your cutting garden in a less conspicuous part of your yard. A true cutting garden is all about production and may not always look perfectly curated. After all, you'll ideally be snipping off the prettiest blooms to use in your arrangements. This garden is not color-coordinated or "landscaped" as

TIPS FOR A GREAT GARDEN LOCATION

- ☐ 12-by-12-foot area
- ☐ Full sun (receives at least six to eight hours a day)
- ☐ Close to water source

far as matching plant forms or creating perfectly spaced plantings. We are trying to get a lot of different kinds of flowers and greens situated in this garden for as much continuous bloom time as possible. Be prepared for times when your garden is quite unruly and growing faster than you can cut, and for times in between growing seasons and may look a bit sparse. It's all part of the cycle of flowers. Keep in mind that the goal is to enjoy these lovelies indoors. Let the garden produce for you, and don't hesitate when it's time to cut the blooming flowers!

ON YOUR MARK, GET SET!

It's helpful when you head outside to your garden to have all the necessary tools and materials at your fingertips. We'll explore how tools can help in creating your garden later in the chapter.

CREATING THE GARDEN

Once you have your tools ready and have identified "the spot," you are ready to make your plans a reality!

Measure out the designated 12-by-12-foot (or whatever size you can accommodate) area in your yard and put stakes in the ground to mark the corners of your space. Tie twine on your stakes along the perimeter so you can easily

OPPOSITE: Before you start digging, it's important to create a garden plan.

RIGHT: Stake off your space and mark off the perimeter with twine.

Garden Supplies

Here's a list of the items I have found necessary, or at least very helpful, in starting a garden:

- Garden journal, for keeping track of your progress. Include plants that you loved or didn't work out, weird weather patterns, and things that you want to remember. A journal is a great way to keep all the information in one place.
- Wheelbarrow or large bucket
- Shovel, for aerating your soil, planting larger plants, etc.
- Rototiller, for soil preparation
- Garden gloves, for hand protection and/or warmth in colder weather
- Rake, for smoothing out the soil or doing general cleanup
- Hoe, for weeding larger swaths of your garden while standing up
- Hand hoe, for weeding while sitting or kneeling. This is great to reach in small areas, such as between individual plants

- Tape measure, to measure your new garden space
- Wood or metal stakes, to stake out your new garden. Metal stakes double as holders for flower netting, if you plan to use it
- Hammer, to insert your stakes
- Twine, to create the borders of your new garden.
- Newspaper or cardboard, for preventing unwanted grass growth in your designated garden area
- Black woven ground cover, for weed control
- Metal staples, to anchor your woven ground cover
- Fertilizers, such as bone meal, fish or seaweed, or general-purpose fertilizer
- Hose, for deep-watering shrubs, etc.
- Watering can, to keep all your new plants properly hydrated
- White flower netting, which is helpful for keeping plants upright in storms and high winds
- Clippers, for harvesting your flowers. Also used for pinching and deadheading (or removing dried, dead blooms from) flowers
- Holster, to have your clippers at the ready but free up your hands while working on other things
- Any plants, seeds, bulbs, etc., that you plan to plant that day
- Plant markers to remember what, where, and when you planted

see the borders of your garden. Next, lay down cardboard or a thick layer of newspaper. (If using newspaper, soak it in water first; it will make handling it easier and will keep it from blowing away.) Cover your cardboard or newspaper with mushroom mulch or compost. Make sure you have enough to provide a thick layer. This combination will kill the grass naturally and will start to feed your soil. You want to build organic matter into your garden and encourage the worms and other beneficial organisms to find a home in your new garden.

You can start this process in either spring or fall. Starting in the fall gives your cardboard/newspaper time to decompose over the winter so that in the spring, you can get going right away. If you start in the spring using this method, you will need to wait out the summer and start your planting in the fall. Fall is a productive time to plant, so it's a great option too.

If you find yourself in the middle of the growing season and just can't wait till fall or the next spring to start, you can do the hard work of digging up the sod or getting a heavy-duty rototiller in there and digging up your ground right away. There's nothing wrong with that! Just be

TOP LEFT: Cardboard is an effective, affordable way to prepare your garden space.

ABOVE: Mulch and compost set the foundation for beneficial organisms.

TOP LEFT: Let time and the elements do their work.

TOP RIGHT: After a few months, your garden will be ready to till.

RIGHT: Break up the ground with a big shovel.

prepared to put some more muscle into it if you're digging by hand.

Once you lay down your cardboard/newspaper and mulch, there's not a lot to do for a few months until it decomposes. Just let winter's harsh rain, sun, wind, cold, and snow do their job to make the materials decompose into a beautiful, organic covering for your garden.

THE BIG DAY

Once a few months have gone by and the cardboard has decomposed, now it's time to dig into the dirt. All your patience has paid off! This is the time to get that soil loosened up. Even though the surface of your garden looks ready to plant, you must get in there with a shovel and dig down so you can aerate (meaning introduce air into) your soil. That ground is most likely very compacted and dense. Just think of your plants' tender roots. They will need to have room to spread out their legs, and if they hit a wall of hard ground, they will struggle to grow. If you take the time to do the hard work of loosening your soil now, before you plant, you will have much better results.

To aerate your soil, take your shovel and dig a section of the garden, ideally digging down about two shovel lengths. This is called double-digging. This should be plenty of depth to give your roots room to spread out. Once this is done, you will have some big clumps of soil to smooth out. Before you take out the rototiller, add

ITEMS TO HAVE ON HAND FOR DIG DAY

- ☐ Garden plan
- ☐ Garden gloves
- ☐ Shovel
- ☐ Compost / mulch
- ☐ Rototiller
- ☐ Rake
- ☐ Wooden stakes
- ☐ Hammer
- ☐ Twine
- ☐ Cardboard
- ☐ Newspaper
- ☐ Tape measure
- ☐ Woven ground cover
- ☐ Staples
- ☐ Propane burner or knife

ABOVE: Remove the original stakes and use the rototiller to mix compost into the soil.

RIGHT: After tilling, add the wooden stakes.

some compost to the soil. Then take the rototiller and till that soil and compost down to an even, level surface. Just think of that mulch, compost, and soil all mixed together to start off your garden with a nutritious base.

If you are unsure about the health of your soil in general, you can always get a soil test done. Depending on your situation, this could also make a huge difference in your success. Ask your local nursery or greenhouse for guidance on what to add to your specific soil. Again, taking the time to do a little homework will pay off in the end. Nothing is more disappointing than spending lots of

RIGHT: A woven ground cover helps with weed control.

BOTTOM LEFT: Staple the ground cover down so it doesn't blow away.

BOTTOM RIGHT: Use more stakes to mark pathways and growing areas.

Having a plan for the weeds will save you from frustration later.

money and time planning your garden but then not having it produce because the soil can't support the plant life.

Next, measure out where your rows will be. It is helpful to have some wooden stakes placed across from each other so you can easily mark off your pathways and growing areas.

Next, if you are using it, you will want to lay down woven ground cover. Lay it down and secure with heavy-duty staples. Once this is in place, you can either cut or burn holes in your plastic for your little plants. I use a propane burner with an attachment and sear the plastic for about one or two seconds. This makes a hole with a hard burnt edge, which I find really helps with fraying. But if all you have is a sharp knife to make a cut in the plastic, that will work too.

If you choose not to use the black plastic, just make sure you have a plan for the weeds that will surely come. At least put down a hefty layer of mulch between your plants. Having a plan for the weeds will save you from frustration later, when the weeds choke out your lovely lisianthus or overtake your perennial section to the point that you don't even know if your plants are in there (believe me, I have lived this scenario).

BELOW: Ready for planting.

PLANTING & CARE

CONDITIONS

When you are finished with the garden preparations, it's time to plant. In preparation for planting, make sure your little plants have been watered and are in good condition. Anytime you plant, it's a shock to that young plant. A healthy, well-watered plant will acclimate much easier and faster to its new home than a weak, dehydrated one.

You can plant on most any day; however, in summer, an overcast day with expected rain in the near future is just about as perfect as you can get. If it's very hot outside, I highly encourage you to plant in the morning (before the heat of the day) or in the evening. This is less stressful and hot for you and the plants.

When I plant, I like to put in a bit of balanced granular fertilizer, specifically made for flowers. In general, make your hole twice the size of the plant's roots. Then tuck in the plant, cover the roots and the rest of the hole with soil, and press firmly. After you get a section done, water with either fish or seaweed solution. Your new plants will love

LEFT Granular fertilizer.

BELOW: Seedlings ready for planting.

ABOVE: I plant my annuals in the plastic ground cover.

this nutrient-dense food, since it helps with transplant shock and encourages early growth. Depending on which type you use, you will just need a pinch to a teaspoon of fertilizer for a small annual. For larger perennials or shrubs, add closer to a tablespoon to the hole. Check your fertilizer bag for specific instructions, since products vary.

When you are planting seeds, you will want to use a sprinkling can when watering so that the seeds don't get washed away. Also, for seeds, there is no need to use any fertilizer until they have sprouted.

Plants are typically broken into three main categories: annual, perennial, or woodie. The annuals get planted in the plastic, the perennials and woodies get planted right in the soil, and the soil gets covered with mulch. I don't cover the perennial/woodie/bulb section of the garden with the plastic ground cover, because I want to give my plants room to expand in that space. I also want to be able to get into the soil to plant my spring-blooming bulbs in the fall.

PLANTING IN THE FALL

In the fall, it's time to plant your bulbs and any perennials that didn't get

TOOLS TO HAVE ON HAND FOR PLANTING DAY:

- ☐ Garden plan
- ☐ Any seeds, bulbs, plugs, or plants you are planting
- ☐ Table knife
- ☐ Hand hoe
- ☐ Granular fertilizer
- ☐ Seaweed or fish fertilizer
- ☐ Watering can
- ☐ Garden gloves
- ☐ Plant labels and permanent marker

planted in the spring. The spring-blooming bulbs—like daffodils, grape hyacinths, hyacinths, tulips and peonies—can be planted only in the fall. This is because the soil is still warm enough to encourage the start of root growth, but the imminent winter and freezing temperatures give the plant its essential rest period.

In general, to plant your bulbs, dig a hole about twice the depth of the bulb, cover the bulbs, and tamp the soil down with the stem facing upward. See the Spring section (page 42) for more specific information by flower type.

Your perennials can be planted in the spring or fall. If I'm able to choose, I typically plant in fall. The temperatures are starting to cool down, and that helps with plant shock as well as keeping the soil a bit wetter. More moisture in the soil keeps the plant from drying out, limiting the need to water so frequently. However, you do need to keep watering about once a week if it's not raining, until the hard freeze. Then when spring rolls around, your plants are ready to start putting on new growth and maybe even flower for you the first year!

One of the keys to success with your cutting garden is to plant your plants at the correct time to give them the best chance at flourishing in your garden. I have consolidated the planting and care schedule later in this chapter so that you can use this as a quick reference for when to complete certain tasks.

Tall Ones in the Back!

Keep in mind that if you include the woodies and evergreens, they should ideally be planted on the north side of the garden. They will eventually get the tallest, and if they are placed where they will give unwanted shade to the rest of the garden, your other plants may have a deficit of sunlight. If you have a hard time identifying a good spot where the trees can be planted on the north side of your garden, you can always plant them elsewhere in the landscape.

WATERING

The best watering comes from a slow, steady, heaven-sent, soaking rain, but you will often need to step in to do the watering yourself. My mom would say something like, "If you want your roots to go deep, water deep." A little sprinkling of water on your plants may make you feel like you've done your job, but if that water is not going down to the roots, it doesn't really help. Water in the early morning, before the heat of the day sets in, or in the evening, after the sun starts to go down. Watering in the morning can be beneficial because it gives the leaves time to dry off during the day. Depending on the plant, wet leaves can lead to mildew (think zinnias, peonies, and dahlias). Watering in the evening is advantageous because the plant has all night to cool down and take a nice long drink, without fear of the sun snatching it away before it's had a chance to benefit the roots. What's better overall—morning or evening? Life gets busy, so we do both. I say, do what's best for your schedule. The main thing is to keep your plants happy and hydrated!

This is when having a hose close to your garden is helpful, but remember: You can use a hose to water established plants, but when watering newly planted seeds, use a watering can or the gentle nozzle on your hose until they sprout. This way, you won't accidentally wash them away.

Once your plants have been in the ground for a few weeks, they are stronger and more established, and you can cut

OPPOSITE: Press firmly once you've tucked the plant in.

RIGHT: Water your plants gently but thoroughly with a watering can before they sprout.

back on watering. Just make sure that your plants are getting at least an inch of rain a week. If not, help them along.

COMPOST

If you don't already compost, even on a very small scale, now is a great time to put those kitchen scraps and leaves to good use! Compost is a nutrient-rich material made up of decaying substances and can be used to nourish your plants. It's basically free and takes just a bit of planning and time but produces wonderful material to feed the soil in your garden. Give it a try!

To get started on your compost pile, you just need a bit of space in the corner of your garden or property. You can dig a hole and throw your clippings in there, or you can construct a bin. My neighbors made their compost bin out of wooden skids. Here at Flourish, we have kind of the Holy Grail of compost bins. It's made from concrete blocks and is broken into three sections. One section is for the "current pile," the place where we put our scraps right now. The second bin is for compost that is currently breaking down. And a third bin is for compost that is ready to be used now. Not everyone has time or space to construct that kind of compost bin, but just about anybody can dig a little hole in the corner of their yard.

Ideally, you want to have your compost pile in a sunny spot so that the sun can help break down the materials. Start with a layer of straw or twigs to help with drainage. Then add layers, alternating between brown and green materials. Brown materials are things like leaves, paper, broken-down cardboard (avoid glossy cardboard and colored papers), sawdust, and straw.

Green materials are things like grass clippings, fruit or veggie scraps, coffee grounds, trimmings from plants, eggshells, and animal manures. If you're lucky enough to live by the ocean, seaweed is great too!

BOTTOM: Make your own compost with a blend of green and brown materials.

WHAT CAN YOU COMPOST?

Green (nitrogen-rich)

- ☐ Manure
- ☐ Tea bags / coffee grounds
- ☐ Fruit and vegetable scraps
- ☐ Grass clippings
- ☐ Egg shells
- ☐ Weeds (with no seeds)
- ☐ Spent flowers / plant clippings

Brown (carbon-rich)

- ☐ Dry leaves
- ☐ Shredded paper / cardboard
- ☐ Wood chips
- ☐ Twigs (break down if too big)
- ☐ Straw
- ☐ Pine needles
- ☐ Dryer lint
- ☐ Pine cones
- ☐ Expired bread, crackers, rice, or pasta
- ☐ Wine corks
- ☐ Wood ashes

Shoot for a ratio of 4 parts brown materials to 1 part green.

Depending on what materials you are using, compost can take anywhere from a few weeks to a year, depending on how quickly the material decomposes. We typically let ours break down for about six to nine months.

Once you start utilizing your own compost, you will be hooked. It's easy to do, and your plants love it! It just takes a little planning, space, and time.

Compost is a nutrient-rich material made up of decaying substances and can be used to nourish your plants. It's basically free and takes just a bit of planning and time.

ONGOING CARE

Having everything planted, watered, and growing is a great feeling, for sure, but there are a few additional things to do that will help your flowers to continue to be healthy and happy.

Pinch Me!

Some annuals benefit from a pinch early on in their development. This helps them produce more usable stems. These

LEFT: Pinching your plants early on can lead to more flowers later.

include snapdragons, dahlias, zinnias, amaranths, and celosia. Simply pinch out the center stem when the plant is about 6 inches tall. This will delay the plant blooming for a week or two, but in the long run, you will have more flowers. Sometimes we leave half the crop to flower naturally, and the other half gets pinched. That way we have a staggered bloom so that it blooms over a longer period. Others, like celosia, should all get pinched because they will produce only one large, slightly obnoxious, unusable head if they are not.

ABOVE: Add Sluggo to the soil to protect against slugs and snails.

Common Diseases and Pests

No one likes to talk about pests and disease, but bugs are certainly out there, and disease can show up, even when you are doing your best to care for your plants. The type of pests and disease you fight will depend on your area, the time of year, and your specific conditions, but below are a few common culprits to be aware of.

Powdery mildew is a disease common to flowers. Peonies, zinnias, and dahlias can all struggle with this nasty fungus. It can stem from high humidity, poor air circulation, or overcrowding, but some flowers are simply prone to this problem. To help ward off this fungus, water in the morning so the plants have time to dry off, and cut the flowers often to keep the plant from growing too large. There are several sprays on the market for powdery mildew as well.

If you notice powdery mildew on a flower you've cut, be sure to discard the cut plant material in the trash (not in your compost) to avoid spreading it around your garden.

Zinnias are also very susceptible to this later in the season. We try to get ahead of this by adding a second or third planting of zinnias. That way, if one planting suffers from powdery mildew, you can still bank on future crops. If you don't have time or space to do that, a spray for fungi is worth a shot.

If our dahlias are struggling, we try to keep them going as long as possible with a weekly application of a fungal spray. Again, when removing the plants from the garden, do not add them to the compost pile, instead disposing of them in your trash.

On the topic of dahlias, let's take a moment to lament about dahlia pests. Dahlias are beautiful and a worthwhile addition to your cutting garden, but they can also be susceptible to aphids, spider mites, thrips, and earwigs. Aphids and thrips can stunt a plant's growth, because they suck on the sap of the plant, depriving it of the nutrients it needs to flourish. A sign of spider mites is yellowed leaves, and earwigs chew on the leaves and petals at night, disfiguring the plant. If you notice problems, start by using a natural, organic solution before immediately jumping to a chemical spray.

Make the Cut

Flowers like lilacs, snapdragons, zinnias, and dahlias like to be deadheaded. If you are regularly cutting your flowers to use

in arrangements, you will naturally be doing this. Win, win! If you get behind on cutting, just try to go out and cut any spent flowers about once a week to keep the flowers coming.

3 MAIN BENEFITS OF DEADHEADING:

- ☐ Improves your plants' appearance
- ☐ Results in more flowers
- ☐ Keeps diseases at bay

YOU DID IT!

So now, take a minute and step back from your garden and admire your work. It's important to celebrate your wins and be proud of what you've planted. With some sun, rain, a little fertilizer, and maybe a little verbal encouragement now and then, your plants are going to grow and reward you with lots of blooms in the coming months.

Next, let's look at each season and dig into the flowers that will give your garden as much continuous bloom as possible.

ABOVE: Your garden may look sparse to start, but soon that will change.

PLANTING and ONGOING CARE SCHEDULE

	January	February	Early March	Late March	Early April	Late April	Early May	Late May	Early Ju
	Order plants, seeds, etc.; plan your garden!								
Hellebore		Cut back old growth, fertilize							
Hyacinth									
Grape Hyacinth									
Daffodil									
Tulip									
Lilac			Fertilize	Plant new plants				Cut back spent blooms	
Allium				Fertilize					
Baptisia									
Peony				Fertilize					
Bachelor's Button				Plant seeds for early summer bloom					
Love-in-a-Mist				Plant seeds for early summer bloom					
Snapdragon					Plant plugs, fertilize		Pinch plants		
Sweet William					Plant plugs, fertilize				
Yarrow					Plant new plants				
Larkspur				Plant seeds for early summer bloom					
Astilbe					Plant new plants, fertilize				
Feverfew					Plant plugs, fertilize				
Lavender				Trim 1/3 old foliage	Plant new plants				
Rudbeckia					Plant plugs, fertilize				
Veronica					Plant new plants, fertilize				
Pin Cushion Flower					Plant new plants, fertilize				
Blue Thistle					Plant new plants				
Lisianthus					Plant plugs, fertilize		Fertilize		Fertilize
Basil							Plant, fertilize		
Zinnia								Plant seeds	
Queen Anne's Lace				Plant seeds for early summer bloom					
Dara Carota								Plant seeds	
Hydrangea			Cut back about 1/3 of plant		Plant new plants				
Strawflower							Plant plugs, fertilize		
Floss Flower							Plant plugs, fertilize		
Amaranthus							Plant plugs, fertilize		
Cockscomb							Plant plugs, fertilize		
Grasses							Plant plugs, fertilize		
Cosmos								Plant seeds	
Sunflower							Plant seeds		
Dahlia							Plant new plants or tubers		Pinch, fer
Eucalyptus					Plant plugs, fertilize				
Anemone					Plant new plants, fertilize				
Sedum					Plant new plants, fertilize				
Cypress					Plant new plants, fertilize				
Juniper					Plant new plants, fertilize				
Winterberry					Plant new plants, fertilize				
Dusty Miller							Plant new plugs, fertilize		

te June	Early July	Late July	Early August	Late August	Early September	Late September	Early October	Late October	November	December
					Feed with compost or fertilizer	Plant new plants				
								Plant bulbs		
								Plant bulbs		
								Plant bulbs		
								Plant bulbs		
								Plant bulbs		
						Plant new plants	Cut back foliage			
						Plant new roots, cut back foliage				
ll out plants to make om for summer seeds					Plant seeds for spring bloom					
ll out plants to make om for summer seeds					Plant seeds for spring bloom					
					Cut back spent blooms					
					Plant seeds for spring bloom					
					Plant new plants					
					Cut back spent blooms					
					Cut back spent blooms					
	Fertilize	Cut back spent blooms	Fertilize							
nch										
					Plant seeds for spring bloom					
nch										
nch										
nch										
nch										
	Fertilize		Fertilize		Fertilize					
					Cut back spent foliage					
					Cut back spent foliage					

HARVESTING SCHEDULE

	3/1 – 3/15	3/16 – 3/31	4/1 – 4/15	4/16 – 4/30	5/1 – 5/15	5/16 – 5/31	6/1 – 6/15	6/16 – 6/30
Hellebore	•	•	•					
Hyacinth				•				
Grape Hyacinth				•				
Daffodil				•	•			
Tulip				•	•			
Lilac				•				
Baptisia						•		
Allium					•			
Peony						•		
Bachelor's Button							•	•
Love-in-a-Mist							•	•
Snapdragon							•	•
Sweet William							•	•
Yarrow						•	•	
Lavender								•
Larkspur							•	•
Astilbe							•	
Feverfew								•
Queen Anne's Lace								•
Rudbeckia								•
Veronica								•
Pin Cushion Flower								•
Blue Thistle								
Lisianthus								
Basil								
Zinnia								
Dara Carota								
Hydrangea							•	•
Strawflower								•
Floss Flower								
Amaranthus								
Cockscomb								
Grasses								
Cosmos								
Sunflower								
Dahlia								
Eucalyptus								
Anemone								
Sedum								
Cypress								
Juniper								
Winterberry								
Dusty Miller								•

7/1 – 7/15	7/16 – 7/31	8/1 – 8/15	8/16 – 8/30	9/1 – 9/15	9/16 – 9/30	10/1 – 10/15	10/16 – 10/31	November	December
•									
•									
•									
•	•	•							
•									
•	•	•	•						
	•	•							
	•	•	•	•					
	•	•	•	•	•	•			
	•	•	•	•	•	•			
	•	•	•	•	•				
•	•	•	•	•	•	•			
•	•	•	•	•	•	•			
•	•	•	•	•	•	•			
•	•	•	•	•	•	•			
•	•	•	•	•	•	•			
•	•	•	•	•	•	•			
•	•	•	•	•	•	•			
•	•	•							
	•	•	•	•	•	•			
		•	•	•	•	•	•	•	•
					•	•			
	•	•	•	•	•				
								•	•
								•	•
								•	•
•	•	•	•	•	•	•	•	•	•

PART TWO

THE FLOWERS

The time has finally come to get into the nitty-gritty of our core flower list. These are flowers I've been growing for many years now, and they are as familiar to me as an old friend.

They are easy to grow, produce, and cut. However, depending on your conditions, climate, and preferences, you may find there are some flowers that don't do as well for you. Look at this as an opportunity to find some new flowers to enjoy. At Flourish, we are constantly on the lookout for better flowers, newer varieties, and unusual but beautiful cutting material. The quest for the perfect garden never ends, but it's a joy to learn and experiment along the way!

GENERAL CONDITIONS

This section covers plant names, types, suggested varieties, and bloom time for each flower. Before we get into that, let's talk about general conditions that all these plants need to grow, as well as some general tips for cutting.

First, your soil should have a general pH of 6.0 to 6.5. This falls slightly inside the acidic range for soil levels, which allows most garden plants to access the nutrients they need to thrive. You can either do this with a home soil test or contact your local USDA Extension Office to come out and do the test for you. All these flowers need full sun, so make sure your garden sits in an area that will get at least six hours of direct sunlight every day.

My test garden is at our property in southeastern Pennsylvania, which is a Zone 6b location. You may need to modify your planting, growing, and harvesting times slightly to suit your zone and location. Ask your local garden club or garden center staff for any specific questions about growing in your zone.

When I talk about adding fertilizer to your hole at planting time, we use a granular fertilizer that looks like little pellets with an even ratio like 5-5-5. You can look for a balanced fertilizer such as Vigoro's Organix Plant Food, or one with a close-to-even ratio, such as Espoma's Organic Flower-Tone Bloom Booster. Each of those numbers corresponds to the nutrients nitrogen, phosphorus, and potassium, respectively. This kind of

One of my former flower-farming instructors often said, "Always put a bit of the ocean in your garden."

fertilizer provides a good, balanced mix of these essential ingredients, giving your baby plant everything it needs to start thriving without any major deficiencies.

One of my former flower-farming instructors often said, "Always put a bit of the ocean in your garden." Fish and seaweed fertilizer are our way of doing

that. They are our preferred method for ongoing fertilizing. Both options are great for plants because they provide a natural source of essential ingredients. Seaweed is high in micronutrients and growth hormones, while fish is high in nitrogen, promoting strong plant growth and healthy soil. All this without any harsh chemicals! If you can, try alternating between these two fertilizers when you feed your plants to get the benefits from both.

HARDENING OFF

In the spring, it's especially important to harden off your plants when you get them home from the nursery. This means that you are trying to acclimate them to being outside full-time after being in their cozy little greenhouse environment. The best way to do this is to choose a day to initially bring them outside that is mild in temperature and not too windy. Let them sit outside, preferably next to a building, to provide a little wind protection for an hour or two the first day. Then bring them inside again. The next day, if it's still mild, let them outside for a few more hours. Continue this for a total of about three to four days and leave them outside, slightly protected (next to a building), for a few nights. Believe me, even though you will be anxious to get your plants in the ground, you will be so glad you took these steps. I have lost many plants due to impatience, and I have learned the hard way not to skip this process.

OPPOSITE: Fertilize your plants regularly to keep them healthy and strong.

TIME TO CUT

And now: a few general tips on cutting.

Unless it is cool outside, we cut our flowers in the early morning or evening. Cutting during the cooler parts of the day helps preserve their moisture content, ensuring they stay fresh and turgid, lasting as long as possible in the vase. Cutting in the heat of the day is hard on the plant; it's already exerting energy by withstanding the heat of the day, so cutting the flower will put more stress on it, causing it to wilt sooner than necessary.

After cutting, put the stems in water as soon as possible and let them sit in a cool, dark place for a couple hours, if possible. This pause gives the flower time

A CUT ABOVE: Best Practices for Cutting Flowers

- ☐ Use a clean, sharp blade—this eliminates tearing or spreading of disease on the plant.
- ☐ Cut in the early morning or evening (not in the heat of the day).
- ☐ Cut on an angle—to allow as much water in the stem as possible.
- ☐ Strip off any leaves that will sit below the waterline.
- ☐ Put cut stems directly into a clean container of water.
- ☐ Let the flowers sit for a few hours to condition before designing with them.

to "condition," or hydrate, after the stress of being cut.

Almost all flowers want you to cut a long stem. This will encourage the new growth of the plant to grow a long stem in return! Cut at a 45-degree angle. The elongated area that this cut creates on the end of the stem allows the flower to take in as much water as possible.

Once you are ready to arrange your flowers, remove all leaves that will be submerged in water, since these soon turn slimy and start to rot. This will contaminate the water and shorten the flower's lifespan. Replacing your water every few days and quickly recutting the last ½ to 1 inch of the stem will help them last longer, as well. If you have access to flower food, stirring that into the water will also help keep the water clean and give your flowers nutrients to stay happier longer.

END GAME

At the end of the season, you will need to get your garden cleaned up. For perennials, this means cutting back the foliage to a few inches above the ground. For annuals, their time is done. Pull out the entire plant and either compost it or put it in the trash. For woodie plants, check my specific instructions on if, how, and when to prune, listed in the individual plant profiles.

BELOW: Your cutting garden may play host to an array of pollinators, like this butterfly.

ABOVE: Tulips in bloom.

SPRING

I live in Lancaster County, Pennsylvania, which is known for its picturesque countryside with lots of Amish and Mennonite farms. When the spring rains come and the fields start to green up after the brown, dried look of winter, it's a feast for the eyes. It's time to get back to tending the land, and we are all very happy to comply!

As we outdoorsy people are well aware, "spring fever" is a real thing! Once the days start to lengthen and the air and sun start to warm the earth, those of us inclined toward gardening are ready to hit the ground running. We are so excited to get busy after long months of planning and dreaming. Once we get into the garden, the smell of the earth (and the first glimpse of bulbs and seedlings emerging) gets us even more energized!

FIRST THINGS

Most likely, the winter has been a little harsh on your garden, so the first order of business is to do some "spring cleaning." Clear away any debris that has blown into your garden, cut back any old growth that wasn't done last fall, pull out any hardy weeds that have found their way into your garden, and add compost to your soil for the coming growing season. These seemingly insignificant tasks will make way for your garden to flourish!

EARLY SPRING CLEANING—
Essential tasks to do in the garden at the very end of winter or the beginning of spring.

- ☐ Clear away debris
- ☐ Cut back old growth
- ☐ Pull out weeds
- ☐ Add compost

SPRING SIGHTINGS!

Spring flowers mostly consist of anything you've planted last fall, such as bulbs, cool-loving annuals, and perennials that have been planted last fall and will make your garden shine!

In early spring, you will be planting some cool-loving annuals, and by late spring, you will be planting your summer and fall annuals. Keep in mind that when you are planting these new babies, you may want to cover them with a frost cloth to give them a little protection against the lingering cold winds.

This is also a good time to add on to your existing garden if you've been wanting to expand your flower space. See the "Getting Started" chapter (page 14) for suggestions on how to break up new ground.

As early spring melts into late spring, the garden is constantly changing and there are new flowers to cut every week. It's time to get out your clippers and start cutting those flowers you so lovingly planted last fall. Don't be shy! Bring those flowers in your house to fully enjoy the fruits of your labor!

SPRING

HELLEBORE

(Helleborus)

PLANT TYPE: Perennial

SUGGESTED VARIETY: "Wedding Party Series"

BLOOM TIME: mid-March – mid-April

We love our hellebores for many reasons, but it certainly doesn't hurt that they are the first ones on the spring flower roster! These perennials, once established, require little care during the year. With just a little attention, these plants will give you what you want so badly: beautiful, early blooms for cutting.

GROWING: Hellebores like to live in well-draining soil with a pH of 6.0 – 7.5. They do require consistent water, especially while they are getting established and during dry periods through the growing months, but don't overwater to the point that they get soggy. Adding compost during planting and once or twice during the growing season is a plus for almost any plant, and these are no exception.

CUTTING TIPS: These plants start to put out flowers sometimes as early as December, depending on the plant. You can certainly cut these anytime they bloom, but in my experience, they last much longer as a cut flower once the stamens and petals fall off and all you have left are the sepals. The sepals are the showy parts of the hellebore, and the stamens and petals are the frilly part of the inside of the bloom. The flower will look a little less full, but you will get a much longer bloom when the stems are cut at this "maturity stage." You can expect these flowers to last one to two weeks in a vase if mature, or one to two days if cutting while they still have stamens.

ADDITIONAL TIPS: Cut back dead or damaged leaves in late winter or early spring. This makes room for the new flowers to emerge and gives the plant the ability to put more energy into the year's new growth. You can fertilize with a light application of a balanced fertilizer in early spring, ideally after you cut back the previous year's growth. We plant our hellebores between our peonies so that when the hot summer sun comes along, they have some shade.

"Wedding Party Series" hellebores

SPRING

HYACINTH
(Hyacinthus)

PLANT TYPE: Bulb

SUGGESTED VARIETIES: "City of Harlem," "Gypsy Queen," "Blue Festival"

BLOOM TIME: Late March – early April

GRAPE HYACINTH
(Muscari armeniacum)

PLANT TYPE: Bulb

SUGGESTED VARIETIES: "Ocean Magic," "White Magic"

BLOOM TIME: Early – mid-April

I haven't come across many people who think of these as cut flowers; I certainly didn't for several years. But once you try them out, you will be happy you did! Both are early bloomers and have a good vase life, as well as cheerful spring colors; what's not to love?

GROWING: Both flowers like well-draining soil. Plant bulbs in mid-to-late fall, about 4 to 6 inches deep for hyacinths and 3 inches deep for grape hyacinths, stem-side-up. Leave just a few inches between bulbs. We allow the naturally occurring rains to water them, but in dry periods, help them along with watering. After they bloom, stop watering and allow them to go dormant. You can leave your grape hyacinth bulbs in the ground for several years to rebloom every spring. If they like where they are, they will multiply and spread. You may need to rein them in if they are too plentiful. If they start to lose their original color or are not performing well, you may need to replant new ones in the fall.

CUTTING TIPS: Hyacinth blooms can last four days to a week. The key is to pull out the whole plant, bulb and all, when harvesting. I know this seems wrong, but by doing this, you will gain a few inches of stem length. We replant new bulbs every year; if you don't want to do that, cut the stem at soil level. Make sure to leave as much of the leaf system as you can to let the bulb take in energy for the next year. Cut grape hyacinth when the flowers are showing good color but before the clusters look spent. We try to cut the longest stem possible, which means cutting into the ground to gain length. They last four to seven days in a vase.

Hyacinth mix, "Ocean Magic" grape hyacinth

SPRING

DAFFODIL

(Narcissus)

PLANT TYPE: Bulb

SUGGESTED VARIETIES: "Cheerfulness," "Gay Tabor," "Bridal Crown"

BLOOM TIME: Late March – late April, depending on type

I remember when a friend first suggested that I grow daffodils to sell at Flourish. I immediately dismissed the idea. I was not a big fan of the traditional yellow trumpets that I knew as daffodils. Fast-forward a few years, and one day a bulb catalog came in the mail that included double daffodils. I didn't even know what I was seeing at first, but I fell in love with them on sight! Although they bloom a little later than "normal" daffodils, they are worth the wait. Long vase life, fluffy petals, and a beautiful scent—they are a winner in every way!

GROWING: These bulbs are also best planted in fall and sown about 4 to 7 inches deep in well-draining soil. Space them about 3 inches apart. They can be left alone to soak in normal rainfall, but you can water if it is a dry period, especially in early spring. Fertilize your bulbs with a bulb food or bone meal at planting time and again in the spring as new growth appears. If you have very good soil, you may find that you can fertilize less. After blooming, leave the foliage uncut so that the plant can gain energy and nutrients for the next year. You can cut off the leaves completely once they turn brown. Daffodils will reward you with numerous years of spring blooms!

CUTTING TIPS: Cut daffodils when the bud is swelling and showing some color. If combining daffodils with other flowers in a vase, let them soak in a bucket for at least an hour before arranging. They will emit "daffodil sap" when they are first cut, which can be harmful to other plants and cause them to wilt prematurely. Leaving them to themselves in their own container of water for a while provides time for the sap to run out of the stem so that it is safe to use them with other flowers. Flowers should last for five to seven days in a vase.

"Gay Tabor" daffodils

SPRING

TULIP

(Tulipa)

PLANT TYPE: Bulb

SUGGESTED VARIETIES: "Foxy Fox Trot," "Apricot Parrot," "Orange Princess," "Charming Beauty," "Mount Tacoma," "Blue Spectacle"

BLOOM TIME: mid-April – early May

Can you tell I had a hard time narrowing down my favorite tulips? Tulips are the very first flower that bloomed at Flourish over 24 years ago, and they will always have a special place in my heart.

When the tulips bloom, spring is in full swing, and you will have more and more things to use in your arrangements. Such a fun time of year for a cut-flower grower!

GROWING: These bulbs also get planted in the fall at a depth of 5 to 6 inches. Plant them very close together, 1 to 2 inches apart. Use bone meal to fertilize when planting and again in the spring as they emerge from the soil. We also cover our bulbs with a few inches of straw to encourage the stems to grow even longer. Most growers may not need to do that, but if you want them to gain a few inches, you can. Just let the rain fall and water your tulips naturally, but, again, if it is a very dry spring, help them along with supplemental watering.

CUTTING TIPS: For the longest-lasting blooms, harvest your tulips when the bud is showing color, and definitely before they fully open. In addition to placing straw over the newly planted bulbs, we also pull these plants, bulb and all, out of the ground to gain more stem length. We plant new bulbs every year, but even if you don't pull out your bulbs every year, I would encourage you to get new bulbs every few years at least. This will give you higher-quality flowers that stay true to their original color. If left in the ground for too many years, tulips start to give smaller blooms and may even revert to the dominant colors for tulips: red and yellow. Flowers should last anywhere from five to twelve days in a vase, depending on the variety and when in their life cycle you cut them.

"Apricot Parrot" tulips

SPRING

LILAC

(Syringa vulgaris)

PLANT TYPE: Woodie

SUGGESTED VARIETY: "Miss Kim"

BLOOM TIME: late April – early May

I really wanted to include this iconic spring flower in the garden plan, but I wasn't sure that I could because these are traditionally very large bushes. How excited I was to discover that breeders are creating new "dwarf" varieties of this longtime favorite garden species, and thus, I give you "Miss Kim"! This variety is supposed to grow only 4 to 6 feet tall, and I would encourage you to keep it well trimmed, closer to 4 feet, if possible. There may come a day when you will need to remove this from your garden if it grows too large. Maybe by then they will have even more varieties of these small lilacs! Either way, this is a beautiful and valuable addition to the backyard cutting garden.

GROWING: Lilacs like well-drained, loamy or sandy soil with a pH of 6.0 to 7.0. Make sure this plant gets watered well once a week through the growing season until it is established for about one year (either by rainfall or by you). Once the bush is established, you shouldn't need to water unless you are experiencing a very dry year. If possible, make this plant one of the first things you put in your garden so that you can dig the hole two to three times the size of the root ball. Fertilize in early spring with a balanced fertilizer to promote a healthier plant and flowers. Deadhead any uncut flowers after it is finished blooming.

CUTTING TIPS: Cut when some of the florets on the flower have bloomed, but not all. There should be quite a few unopened buds at the top of the flower. Because the stem is wood, I like to smash or cut up the length of the stem about 4 inches or so to allow the branch to more easily take up water.

"Miss Kim" lilac

SPRING

ALLIUM

(Allium sativum)

PLANT TYPE: Bulb

SUGGESTED VARIETY: "Purple Sensation," "Ambassador"

BLOOM TIME: Early – mid-May

This unique plant, part of the onion family, creates perfectly round heads on leafless stems, which might explain why I call it the "Dr. Seuss flower." To me, it looks like something a child would imagine and draw on paper. Its purple, white, or blue flowers are a fun addition to spring bouquets. I think I really began to love this flower when I realized that it bloomed right over Mother's Day.

GROWING: This flower is easy to grow. Plant the bulbs in the fall; depth of planting depends on the size of the bulb. You want to plant them about twice as deep as the bulb is tall, usually about 4 to 6 inches deep. Cover with soil and water after planting, but let the fall and winter rains water the bulbs naturally. These bulbs can come back on their own for several years and typically you don't need to fertilize them, but if needed, you can fertilize with a balanced fertilizer in late summer to encourage better blooms the following spring.

CUTTING TIPS: Cut allium when the florets are mostly open and vibrant in color. Just be aware that because these blooms are directly related to onions, they can emit a potent, onion-like fragrance right after cutting. Allium also tend to color the water with a pink-purple pigment. For this reason, I prefer to arrange them in a galvanized vase or a ceramic vessel. They should last in your arrangement for one week, but some have been known to last even longer!

Purple-toned allium

SPRING

BAPTISIA or WILD INDIGO

(Baptisia australis)

PLANT TYPE: Perennial

SUGGESTED VARIETY: "Lunar Eclipse"

BLOOM TIME: End of May – mid-June

The long and delicate look of this flower just woos me! This variety, "Lunar Eclipse," is my favorite. The bottom of the flower starts out as a soft lavender color and then fades to white at the tip. This flower looks great in all sorts of arrangements, but I think the best way to enjoy it is just a few stems in a vase by themselves.

GROWING: Plant this perennial in the spring or fall in well-drained, loamy or sandy soil. Just make sure that it's where you want it because, unlike a lot of perennials, this one is difficult to replant. It's tough to dig out once established. Dig a hole about twice the size of your container. Avoid planting it too deep, since this can cause root rot.

This plant is pretty hardy on its own, but you can give it some balanced fertilizer in the spring as new growth emerges, if needed. Deadhead any spent flowers after they bloom. Then, in the fall, cut the plant back to the ground for the winter. This plant can take longer than you think to emerge in the spring. So, don't be worried if new growth doesn't surface for a while. It grows quickly once it starts, and you will get blooms in just a few weeks!

CUTTING TIPS: Cut the flowers when about half the florets have opened. Flowers should last about seven to ten days, depending on the stage at which they are cut. The uncut blooms will produce seedpods, which can be fun to design with. We also like to use the foliage in our arrangements. This plant will give you something to cut, whether it's flowers, pods, or greens, for much of the growing season!

"Lunar Eclipse" baptisia

SPRING

PEONY

(Paeonia)

PLANT TYPE: Tuber

SUGGESTED VARIETIES: "Coral Charm," "Festiva Maxima"

BLOOM TIME: Mid-May – early June

I couldn't do a cut-flower garden without peonies. I love their big, fluffy blooms. Sometimes when we are cutting large armloads of them, I think I would like to make a bed out of them, lie down, and take a nap in all their goodness!

GROWING: In the fall, plant tubers about 2 to 3 inches deep, and about 18 inches to 2 feet apart. They do best in well-drained, fertile soil. Add some compost to the soil when you plant and in the spring. You could also use a balanced, slow-release fertilizer in the early spring, when new growth emerges, but you may not need to, since peonies are pretty self-sufficient if they are happy. Deadhead spent blooms. In the fall, cut back the plants to a couple inches to overwinter.

Peonies are known for getting a gray mold as the season progresses. Don't be alarmed. Just cut back the stems and put them into your trash. Do not add them to your compost, since this can spread the mold to your other plants!

CUTTING TIPS: Usually by this time of the year, you'll get some very warm days. Cutting in the early morning or early evening will give your flowers a better vase life, because they will not be taxed by the sun's heat. Cut the bloom at "marshmallow stage." It should be showing color and still mostly unfurled, but squishy. Once you harvest a few, you'll know exactly what that means. Flowers should last five to seven days, depending on the stage at which they are cut.

ADDITIONAL TIPS: Many people have asked me about the notorious ants that crawl on the blooms. I can honestly say that we haven't had many problems with that, but I tell people to cut them in the early morning (or evening) and, if you see any ants, to take your stems of peonies and lightly but firmly bang them on the ground to shake any lingering ants off. You can also try briefly submerging the flower heads in a bucket of clean water.

Various peonies

SPRING

BACHELOR'S BUTTON

(Centaurea cyanus)

PLANT TYPE: Annual grown from seed

SUGGESTED VARIETIES: "Frosty Mix," "Jazzy Mix"

BLOOM TIME: Mid-May – mid-June

Anytime you can grow a blue flower, you should! These annuals, planted as seeds, are one of the first to bloom, often coinciding with the last peonies. They lend a great wildflower look to your arrangements with their sweet little faces. They are easy to grow from seed and will often reseed from year to year if left unchecked. Try sowing these in early fall to get them to bloom even earlier in the spring.

GROWING: Sow seed directly in well-drained soil in early fall or early spring. We sort of pinch the seeds between our fingers and spread them as we go. The seeds are tiny, so don't try to individually plant each one. Plant seed about ¼ inch deep and cover lightly with soil. Keep the soil consistently moist until established, but don't water too much—you don't want your seeds to rot! We find that one or two deep waterings a week is sufficient as long as it's not too dry. You don't need to fertilize bachelor's buttons.

Once the plants have their first two "true leaves," you can thin out the plants to give the existing ones more space. If you don't do this step, it can lead to weaker plants because they don't have the space for a proper root base. They will need that to withstand the summer winds and storms.

CUTTING TIPS: Cut when the flower is partially to mostly open. Continually cutting will encourage more to grow. You can also dry them by cutting flowers that are fully opened and hanging them upside down in a cool, dry place. Fresh flowers should last about five to seven days in a vase, depending on the stage at which they were cut.

Blue bachelor's buttons

SUMMER

By the time summer rolls around in your garden, things will be growing rapidly and your garden will be brimming with flowers! Tubers, perennials, and annuals (from seeds and plugs) are all blooming. This allows many options for cut flowers, so keep the arrangements flowing!

This is also the time to keep an eye on watering. If you are not getting consistent, soaking rain on a weekly basis, you will need to be out there with your watering can or hose to make sure everything is either getting off to a good start or has consistent moisture to grow well to maturity.

Take note: This is the likely time when insects or disease can become a problem. Inspect your plants often for signs of munching bugs or mildew. If you get ahead of these problems, it will help you tremendously.

A plant that is heathy will ward off most bugs and diseases, but, in our experience, there are times we just need to give our plants a little help and protection against these formidable foes! My personal philosophy is to always try to make healthy plants a priority by using organic and natural means and materials and using chemicals only when I have no other alternative. Your land, flowers, and future generations will thank you!

The Flourish garden in early summer

SUMMER

LOVE-IN-A-MIST

(Nigella)

PLANT TYPE: Annual grown from seed

SUGGESTED VARIETIES: "Miss Jekyll Double Mix," "Moody Blues"

BLOOM TIME: Early – mid-July

Another beautiful blue wildflower, nigella is another must-have for numerous reasons. It's an early-summer bloomer; it has a beautiful, soft color; and, to top it off, the unused flowers magically become gorgeous seedpods!

GROWING: Sow seed directly in well-drained soil in early fall or early spring. We sort of pinch the seed between our fingers and spread it as we go. The seeds are tiny, so don't try to individually plant each one. Plant seed about ¼ inch deep and cover lightly with soil and softly tamp down to make sure the seeds make contact with the soil. Keep the soil moist until shoots appear. We find that one or two deep waterings a week is sufficient as long as it's not too dry. No need to fertilize; they are fine on their own.

Once the plants have their first two "true leaves," you can thin out the plants to give the existing ones more space. If you skip this step, it can lead to weaker plants because they don't have the root base they need to withstand wind and the elements.

CUTTING TIPS: Cut when the flowers are about half open, when they start to show vibrant color. Wait to cut seedpods until they are fully developed with a nice, deep-red stripe. Hang to dry in bunches in a cool, dry place.

"Miss Jekyll Double Mix" nigella

SUMMER

SNAPDRAGON

(Antirrhinum majus)

PLANT TYPE: Annual from plug

SUGGESTED VARIETIES: "Madam Butterly," "Opus," "Potomac"

BLOOM TIME: late May – early July

I love seeing a whole row of snapdragons blooming. The texture and color and those beautiful spikes just make you want to get out there and capture their sweet goodness to bring them inside! They make a great addition to any arrangement, whether you use them as a short addition to highlight their textural peaks or to fully appreciate them as a tall flower to add drama and height to your floral masterpiece.

GROWING: Plant these in mid-spring, before the last frost date. With a little protection, these plants actually thrive in the cold spring temperatures. In fact, if planted too late in the spring, they will not develop well in summer temperatures. After planting, just give them a little protection with a bit of row cover to keep the wind at bay.

When you put them in the soil, dig a hole a little larger than the root area. Pinch in a little balanced fertilizer to help give the roots nutrients for the months ahead. We like to water with fish or seaweed fertilizer at planting time, and then once a week after that, if possible. Once the weather has stabilized, remove the row cover. When the plant is about 4 to 6 inches tall, it's time to pinch! Pinching out the top 1 to 2 inches of the central stem, just above a leak node. This encourages the plant to send out side shoots, which ultimately gives you more flowers!

CUTTING TIPS: Cut flowers when about ⅓ of the lower buds have opened and they are showing good color. Waiting till all the blooms on the stem have opened decreases vase life.

"Opus" snapdragons

SUMMER

SWEET WILLIAM

(Dianthus barbatus)

PLANT TYPE: Annual from plug

SUGGESTED VARIETY: "Sweet Series"

BLOOM TIME: Mid-June – mid-July

A relative to carnations, these flowers are not the showiest in the garden, but we love their mounded heads of red, white, and pink, and they are a great addition to any bouquet, providing great texture and color. They are easy to grow and may even bloom again for you later in the season, if left in the ground.

GROWING: These flowers are grown from a plug. Plant at the same time as your snapdragons and other spring-planted annuals. Make a hole a little larger than the roots, add some balanced granular fertilizer, and fill. We like to water with fish or seaweed fertilizer at planting time and then once a week, if possible. You can also pinch these plants to encourage more blooms. Pinch when the plant is about 6 to 8 inches tall and has at least four to six sets of leaves. Take off the top 1 or 2 inches of the main stem above a set of leaves.

CUTTING TIPS: Cut sweet William when the flowers are almost all open. Cut as long a stem as you can, since these tend to be shorter plants.

"Sweet Series" sweet William

SUMMER

YARROW

(Achillea millefolium)

PLANT TYPE: Perennial

SUGGESTED VARIETIES: "Moonshine," "Pomegranate," "Sassy Summer Sorbet"

BLOOM TIME: Late May – mid-June

We love a plant that takes very little care and provides reliable flowers. That's yarrow for you! This perennial comes in a variety of colors, and it seems that new varieties are released every year! It's a great filler addition to bouquets or arrangements, giving a nice burst of color on its beautiful umbel-shaped blooms. Those little clusters of flowers are technically called "corymbs" and give yarrow its unique look. It's a quiet workhorse in your garden. Ours have been known to give up to twenty to thirty stems per plant once mature and happily situated.

GROWING: Plant this in the spring or fall, digging the hole about two times the size of the root ball. Plant in soil with a bit of balanced fertilizer, but, as stated, this plant does not need a lot to keep it happy. In the fall, cut back the plant to about 2 to 3 inches to overwinter. You can give it fertilizer again in the spring if you think it's necessary. You may need to replace your plants after a few years if you notice that it has slowed down production.

CUTTING TIPS: Cut when the flower is fully colored. It will not continue to open once it is cut, so make sure it's at the stage you want it when you harvest it.

Yellow yarrow

SUMMER

LARKSPUR

(Delphinium consolida)

PLANT TYPE: Annual grown from seed

SUGGESTED VARIETY: "QIS Series"

BLOOM TIME: June – mid-July

One of my favorite flowers, larkspur is another great one to just gather a bunch and put in a beautiful, tall vase. Related to its even more showy relative, delphinium, it has the same tall, spiky shape but is a little slimmer. Colors range from white and pink to smokey purple, dark violet, and blue.

GROWING: Plant seeds, preferably in the fall for the next spring, although you can plant in early spring and have a nice harvest. If planted in the fall, it will allow for taller plants and earlier bloom, which is optimal. Pinch and spread the seeds on well-loosened soil, and then cover lightly with more soil. Tamp down to ensure the seeds have contact with the soil and water well, taking care not to wash away the seeds. Water one or two times a week until plants start to emerge, usually up to a month or so later. They take some time, so don't be discouraged if they don't come up right away. Make sure to thin out the little seedlings that come up. You want to give these plants space to spread their roots, so give them an inch or two to themselves. Water deeply once a week until well established or during dry periods. There is no need for much fertilizer. A little compost with the soil may just do it. You could use a seaweed or fish fertilizer to ensure you get plenty of blooms. These tend to reseed by themselves, so you may need to rein them in to keep them in one area.

CUTTING TIPS: Cut larkspur when the bottom flowers are starting to open and up to about halfway up the stem. I like to see the top 2 to 3 inches of buds still closed. This is another great textural flower. If you cut when the buds are fully open, you will reduce the vase life.

Larkspur is also great for drying, so take a few extras, bunch them together, and hang them upside down in a cool, dry place. The darker ones keep their color best!

"QIS Series" larkspur

SUMMER

ASTILBE or FALSE GOAT'S BEARD

(Astilbe)

PLANT TYPE: Perennial

SUGGESTED VARIETY: "Visions in Pink"

BLOOM TIME: June

Astilbe is another low-maintenance, workhorse perennial that, once established, happy, and healthy, can produce fifteen to twenty stems per plant. I love it for its feathery and airy spikes of white, pink, or purple flowers. They add so much to a bouquet with their unique texture and form. There are varieties that like more shade, so make sure you choose a variety that can take at least six hours of sun.

GROWING: Plant these in spring or fall, making the hole about twice the size of the root ball. Sprinkle at bit of balanced fertilizer and/or compost in the hole and cover. Water well. Astilbe can benefit from a bit of fertilizer in the spring, when new growth appears, but overfertilizing can result in too many greens and not enough flowers.

Our plants have been growing strong for a number of years now, but I do notice that some years result in more flowers than others. This could be from more or less rainfall depending on the year. Cut back the plant to just above ground level in the fall to make room for new growth in the spring.

CUTTING TIPS: Cut astilbe in the "mid-bloom" stage; you want about half the flowers to be blooming but the top of the flower still closed. This will give you longer vase life. You can also use the flowers in dried arrangements. Simply leave the flower to dry on the plant and cut when they are still colorful and slightly pliable.

"Visions in Pink" astilbe

SUMMER

FEVERFEW

(Tanacetum parthenium)

PLANT TYPE: Annual from plug

SUGGESTED VARIETIES: "Double Tetra White," "Vegmo," "Sunny Ball," "Virgo"

BLOOM TIME: Late June – mid-July

This understated flower will always have a place in my cutting garden. The plant has a branching habit, with shoots of dainty little flowers on each stem. It's a great filler flower that I wish would bloom all year. However, sometimes it does come back to flower at the end of the season if left in the ground, although much less dramatically than in the spring. You will love this in your bouquets!

GROWING: To plant, dig a hole a little larger than the root ball and put in a pinch of balanced fertilizer. Cover and water well. We like to use fish or seaweed fertilizer after planting. You shouldn't need to fertilize during the growing season. Plants can be put in the ground in early spring; they like the cold weather and prefer to get established early. They just need a bit of wind protection in the form of white ground cover. Leave it on until the weather has stabilized (usually mid-spring).

If you have the space, you can cut back the plant to encourage it to rebloom later in the season, but if you are low on space, it's not worth it. In my experience, the rebloom is minimal.

CUTTING TIPS: Cut feverfew when the flowers are fully opened; they will not continue to open very much after you cut. You can dry these by gathering the stems in small bunches and hanging them upside down in a cool, dry space.

"Double Tetra White" feverfew

SUMMER

LAVENDER

(Lavandula)

PLANT TYPE: Perennial

SUGGESTED VARIETIES: "Phenomenal," "Hidcote"

BLOOM TIME: Mid – late June (sometimes re-blooms in fall)

Lavender often evokes a lot of emotion and memories. The smell, the color, the sight of a long row in bloom—somewhere in the conversation about lavender there is usually a contented sigh to be heard. Here at Flourish, we love to grow the deeper purple lavenders so that we can get good color when drying the flowers. But there are many kinds on the market, even a white one! Because the stems only grow to a length of about a foot, fresh lavender is best used in shorter arrangements. It's always a treat to see it tucked away in a vase on the kitchen table, where one can especially enjoy the scent.

GROWING: Plant in the spring, after the last hard frost. Dig a hole twice the width and depth of the base, in a spot with well-drained soil. You can even mix a little handful of sand into the soil during planting. Water after planting and keep watering as it gets established, about once a week. After that, lavender likes to get a little dry. No need to fertilize: this plant is quite content without it! Cut back either after flowering in late summer or in the early spring, avoiding the woody part of the plant. Lavender flowers grow best from the green part of the plant, so cut back about one-third of the stem length to encourage new growth.

CUTTING TIPS: Lavender is ready to cut when the buds show vibrant color and are open almost all the way. To harvest, cut the green stems, avoiding the hard, woody growth. I like to gather a handful of stems in my hand and then make a big cut to harvest several at once. If using the stems for fresh arrangements, place directly into water and let them sit for an hour or two before arranging. If you are planning on drying your lavender, bunch the stems with rubber bands and hang upside down in a dry, dark, airy room for about two weeks.

Pale-purple lavender

SUMMER

BLACK-EYED SUSAN

(Rudbeckia hirta)

PLANT TYPE: Annual from plug

SUGGESTED VARIETIES: "Cherokee Sunset," "Gloriosa Double Daisy," "Irish Eyes," "Indian Summer"

BLOOM TIME: Mid-June – mid-July

Normally, I'm not a huge fan of dark-yellow-and-black flowers, but there are so many beautiful variations of this annual that even I have learned to love it. Many people are familiar with the perennial black-eyed Susans, but I encourage you to look at the annual varieties. Their stems are better suited to cutting, and if you want to try a new variety every year, you can!

GROWING: Plant your plugs in the spring, a few weeks before the last frost date. These plants also like to get established in the cold, so give them a little protection from the harsh winds with row cover until they are well established and the weather has stabilized, which is usually in mid-spring. Dig a hole a little wider that the root ball, place a little fertilizer in the hole, and cover with soil. Water with fish or seaweed fertilizer, if you have it, and then continue to water at least once a week until established.

CUTTING TIPS: The best stage to cut rudbeckia is when the flowers have just fully opened. You don't want to cut too early (when the petals are still tight) or too late (when the flower has already been in bloom for a few days). Obviously, it's hard to tell how long the flower has been opened, but if the flower looks weathered versus clean and vibrant, that can be an indication.

"Cherokee Sunset" and "Indian Summer" black-eyed Susan

SUMMER

VERONICA

(Veronica spicata)

PLANT TYPE: Perennial

SUGGESTED VARIETY: "Royal Candles"

BLOOM TIME: Early June – mid-July

This little-known gem lends a great fuzzy texture and unique shape to your bouquets. It's one of those flowers that doesn't scream for attention but makes your bouquets and arrangements stand out.

GROWING: Plant this perennial in spring or fall in well-drained soil. Dig a generous hole and place some balanced fertilizer in the hole before you close it up. Water after planting and then once a week, and during dry spells, until you are sure it's established. Veronica doesn't take a lot of attention, with minimal need for fertilizer, but you may notice that after a few years the plants get tired and may need to be replaced. In the fall, cut the plant back to the ground.

CUTTING TIPS: Cut the flowers when the top is fully opened but the bottom flowers are still in bud. Cut as long as you can for greater stem length. This perennial has been known to rebloom later in the season, although not as fully as the first flush.

"Royal Candles" Veronica

SUMMER

PINCUSHION FLOWER

(Scabiosa)

PLANT TYPE: Annual from plug

SUGGESTED VARIETIES: "Pincushion Mix," "Scoop"

BLOOM TIME: Late June – mid-July

When I first starting growing cut flowers, I included perennial scabiosa and fell out of love with them pretty quickly. The short stems were wiry and unpredictable, and they produced a small number of flowers that weren't stunning. Years later, I discovered there was an annual scabiosa, and I haven't been without them since. The annual variety produces as many as twenty to fifty stems per plant! The flowers are bigger and come in so many amazing colors. And sometimes, with consistent cutting, they even rebloom after their first flush. If you can get your hands on any of the upscale "Scoop" varieties, do it! The flowers come in a wider color palette, are bigger and fuller, and have more of a rounded head. They are the very best of scabiosa and will make your arrangements sing.

GROWING: You can plant these outside before the last frost; they like the cool weather! Just be sure to use row cover so they have a little protection as they get established. You can also wait until after the frost date to plant. Dig a hole a little larger than the root ball, place some fertilizer in the hole, and cover. Water with fish or seaweed fertilizer after planting and once a week before they bloom, if possible.

CUTTING TIPS: The best stage to cut these flowers is when the heads are fully opened and you see that adorable little pincushion center with the florets circling it. Cut long stems to encourage the plant to rebloom. You can also dry scabiosa by gathering it in bunches and hanging it upside down for a couple weeks.

"Scoop, Focal Red Velvet" scabiosa

SUMMER

BLUE THISTLE

(Eryngium)

PLANT TYPE: Perennial

SUGGESTED VARIETY: “Blue Hobbit”

BLOOM TIME: Mid-July – late July

Here’s another blue flower to love! This prickly plant is worth a spot in your garden and floral arrangements. It’s low maintenance, has a great silvery-blue color, is a long-lasting cut flower, and works great as a dried flower as well. There are more varieties continually coming on to the market, so have fun finding the one you like best.

GROWING: Plant in spring or fall in well-drained soil. Dig your hole to about twice the size of the root ball. Blue thistle prefers sandier soil to heavy clay soil, so add some compost and coarse sand (70% compost, 30% sand) to your soil if you need to lighten it up. Add some balanced fertilizer to your hole, cover, and water. These plants do quite well without fertilizer and even do better without it most of the time. Another reason to love it! Cut back to the ground in fall.

CUTTING TIPS: Cut when the flowers are fully open and have a nice blue color. When harvesting and stripping the leaves of this plant, it’s preferable to use garden gloves. It is truly a thistle and can be a painful experience with bare hands.

To dry, gather it in bunches and hang in a cool, dry place for a couple weeks.

“Blue Hobbit” blue thistle

SUMMER

LISIANTHUS

(Eustoma grandiflorum)

PLANT TYPE: Annual from plug

SUGGESTED VARIETIES: "Caleb," "Rosita," "Voyage"

BLOOM TIME: Mid-July – mid-August

Just about everyone I know who has grown lisianthus is completely in love with it. I tell our brides that I love them even more than roses for a wedding bouquet. They have the same gorgeous, delicate look as a rose, last one to two weeks in a vase, and do well out of water for a decent amount of time. You can actually drop them on the floor and they still look good as new! Definitely a top-notch cut flower!

GROWING: Some people have difficulty growing these, but once you understand what they like, they are not difficult. The key is to be patient; they take a long time to mature. Start your plugs outside in early spring. They need the cooler weather to get well established. Plant them in soil that is well drained and amended with compost. These plants do like to feed, so put some fertilizer in the hole at planting time, and then water with fish or seaweed fertilizer and continue to do that once a week. As stated before, they are slow growers. We try to plant ours in early April but don't see any flowers until mid-July. That's a pretty long time to wait, but it's worth it! We have had years when we had a nice second flush in September. Cut your plants back hard as soon as you can after the first flush, continue to fertilize, and hope for the best!

CUTTING TIPS: Cut lisianthus when the buds are still closed but are showing good color. If the buds are too tight, they will not open after you cut. You'll quickly recognize which stage is too tight or just right! They last a long time in the vase—typically seven to fourteen days!

"Caleb" lisianthus

SUMMER

BASIL

(Ocimum basilicum)

PLANT TYPE: Annual from plug

SUGGESTED VARIETIES: "Cardinal," "Genovese"

BLOOM TIME: July – October

Basil was probably not the first thing you thought of when you dreamed about a cut-flower garden, but it is a great addition nonetheless. It's great as a foliage in your arrangements, and "Cardinal" produces a cluster of dark red bracts that look like bushy flowers. Plus, if you need extra basil for that bruschetta you're making, you can snip some from your cutting garden! The smell of basil is also a great bonus.

GROWING: Basil is very sensitive to temperature, so plant your plugs in late spring, once the frost has passed. Dig your hole a little larger than the root ball, add a little fertilizer, and cover. Water with fish or seaweed liquid fertilizer and continue to water or fertilize once a week, especially if it's a dry season.

CUTTING TIPS: Cut basil in the morning, if possible, and get into water as soon as you can. Basil is more sensitive than most cuts and can be prone to wilting if it's taxed by hot weather or being out of water too long. If it's healthy and cut properly, it can last at least three to five days in the vase.

"Genovese" basil

SUMMER

ZINNIA

(Zinnia elegans)

PLANT TYPE: Annual grown from seed

SUGGESTED VARIETIES: "Benary's Giant Series," "Queeny Lime"

BLOOM TIME: Early July – late September

This was probably one of the first flowers you thought of when you imagined a cut-flower garden, and for good reason! They are easy to grow, and their cheery faces are in just about every summer garden bouquet. Zinnias are loved by many because they are so easy to grow, and they come in a wide variety of colors. Here at Flourish, we love the Queeny Lime series, which includes the unique blush/antique/peach colors that are popular in weddings right now.

GROWING: To grow zinnias, seed them right into the ground after the threat of frost has passed, about ¼ to ½ inch deep. These seeds are a little bigger, so you can place seeds singularly or by twos (to make sure at least one comes up) in the ground about 3 to 4 inches apart. This will eliminate the need to thin later. Cover with soil and water. Seeds should appear in about seven to ten days. Water about once a week, preferably at the base of the plant and in the morning, to give the plants time to dry off. Zinnias are prone to powdery mildew, which many zinnia growers eventually experience in the season. Keeping the leaves dry will help stave it off for as long as possible.

CUTTING TIPS: Cut zinnias when they are fully opened and showing good color. Cut low on the plant so that you get long stems to encourage longer regrowth. Don't be afraid to cut off new buds to get long stems. Continue to deadhead unused flowers to encourage more to grow.

"Benary's Giant Series" zinnia

SUMMER

FALSE QUEEN ANNE'S LACE

(Ammi majus)

PLANT TYPE: Annual from seed

SUGGESTED VARIETY: "Select White"

BLOOM TIME: Early June – mid-July

CHOCOLATE LACE FLOWER or "DARA"

(Daucus carota)

PLANT TYPE: Annual from plug

SUGGESTED VARIETY: "Purple Kisses"

BLOOM TIME: Late June – early August

White and lacy, false Queen Anne's lace gives a dreamy, light touch to anything it sits next to. Dara, its close relative, has the same characteristics but with dark red/purple tones. It's so lovely for bouquets that need a delicate touch of dark color. You can seed this all through the growing season to get longer bloom time if you have the space.

GROWING: Plant the false Queen Anne's lace seed directly in well-drained soil in early spring, as soon as you can get it in the ground. The seeds are very small, so pinch them between your fingers and spread as you go along your row. Cover lightly with soil and tamp down to make sure the seed has made contact. Water well, being careful not to wash away the seed from its place. (Dara, on the other hand, we often grow from plugs, but you can also grow these from seed.)

For both plants, continue watering once or twice a week until the seeds sprout, then once a week in dry periods. Thin the seedlings once they have grown 2 to 4 inches tall. You want them to be about 10 to 12 inches apart. You can give a light application of well-balanced fertilizer, but most likely it will be fine without. If you want, you can also do an early fall planting for an earlier spring harvest.

CUTTING TIPS: Cut false Queen Anne's lace when the flowers are fully white; they will not continue to open once cut. Be aware that this plant can cause skin irritation for some people, so if you are sensitive, wear long sleeves while cutting. Cut Dara when the head is fully developed and the flowers are fully colored. If you cut this too soon, it will not continue to open in the vase. Keep plants deadheaded to encourage new blooms.

"Select White" false Queen Anne's lace; purple-toned Dara

FALL

Fall is one of my favorite seasons. Even though we are still so busy with weddings and events here at Flourish, once the frost hits, it feels like the push of the garden tasks starts to slow down and we can enjoy the beautiful weather and a little bit of a slower pace.

Fall is the time to clear out the year's old growth but also make way for the coming spring. Trim back old growth on your perennials, pull out spent annuals, plant early-spring seeds, and even plant a cover crop to feed your soil over the months where there isn't anything growing in the garden.

If we know a frost is coming, we plan ahead and gather as many flowers as we can. It's a shame to see some cutting-flower favorites, like dahlias, end their season.

This is another good time to enlarge your garden. Using the cardboard-and-mulch method of starting a new area is great to do in the fall!

Fall is also a time to play with any flowers that you've dried over the season. See the "Projects" chapter for a simple dried-flower wreath (page 178). I recommend *Designing with Dried Flowers* by Hannah Rose Rivers Muller if you are interested in dried flower projects. Several of the flowers she suggests for drying are also covered in this book.

Creating a fall-flower-focused backdrop.

FALL

HYDRANGEA

(Hydrangea paniculata)

PLANT TYPE: Woodie

SUGGESTED VARIETIES: "Bobo" or "Little Lime"

BLOOM TIME: Mid-July – late October

Years ago, I went to a cut-flower conference. The speaker said that if you had to invest in just one flower at your farm, it should be "Limelight Hydrangea." It's so easy to grow, it's a reliable bloomer, and it changes color from lime green to white to pink and then burgundy, all beautifully timed according to the season. Now, almost 25 years later, I would still have to agree! And good news for you home gardeners: This monstrous shrub now comes in a dwarf variety, "Little Lime," or a similar one called "Bobo." You will love how this vigorous plant repays you with flowers almost all season for years to come.

GROWING: Plant in early spring or fall in lightly acidic, well-drained soil (pH 5.5 to 7.0) in a hole that's about twice the size of the root ball. You can add a balanced, slow-release fertilizer to the soil. Fill the hole with soil and water well. Prune in late winter or early spring, before new growth appears. Cut back to about ⅓ the size of the plant to encourage growth and abundant flowers! Remove any dead or damaged wood as well.

CUTTING TIPS: Cut flowers when they are fully opened and look fresh and firm. Leave at least half the flowers on the plant so that it doesn't tax the plant too much and gives it energy to bloom next season. Flowers should last at least seven to ten days in the vase. To dry hydrangeas, cut when they are fully developed, usually in late summer or early fall. Place a few stems in a vase with a small amount of water and out of the sun. Let them take up the water, but do not replenish when it's gone. They will naturally and gradually dry in the vase like this. Once dry, you can try spraying them with hairspray to keep them from shattering easily.

"Little Lime" hydrangea

FALL

STRAWFLOWER

(Xerochrysum bracteatum)

PLANT TYPE: Annual from plug

SUGGESTED VARIETY: "King Series"

BLOOM TIME: Mid-June – mid-October

Strawflowers are a beautiful curiosity with their paperlike petals. They add a great wild aesthetic to your garden and do well as fresh flowers, but they really shine as dried flowers too. With some consistent cutting, they will continue to bloom all season long.

GROWING: Plant these in early to late spring. They can handle the cold weather with a little wind protection from row cover. You can also wait to plant these until the weather has stabilized, and up until early summer. Dig a hole twice the size of the root ball and put a pinch of balanced fertilizer in the hole. Cover with soil, and water with fish or seaweed fertilizer.

CUTTING TIPS: Cut when the flowers are fully opened but before the center yellow part gets too enlarged. They should last about seven to ten days in the vase. To dry, you can bunch and hang them in a cool, dry location. If you just want the head (and not the stems), you can cut the head off right where the stem and flower meet, and put the head on a straight wire. You can use them right away like this, since the heads are essentially already dry.

"King Series" strawflowers

FALL

FLOSS FLOWER

(Ageratum houstonianum)

PLANT TYPE: Annual from plug

SUGGESTED VARIETY: "Blue Horizon"

BLOOM TIME: Mid-June – frost

Talk about a flower that wants to produce! This little wonder may not look like much but we love it for its hardworking nature. Truly, the more you cut it, the more it blooms. However, be warned that if you neglect cutting this plant, it will start to look ugly and will not produce any more flowers. You really must keep cutting this plant consistently to benefit from its constant flowers. This blue flower is a great addition to other vibrant colored flowers but also looks great with whites and greens.

GROWING: Plant this annual after the danger of frost has passed, in late spring or early summer. Plant in a hole twice the size of the roots, put a pinch of balanced fertilizer in the hole, and cover with soil. Water with fish or seaweed fertilizer. This hard worker doesn't need continual fertilizer through the season, but you can give it a boost once in a while if you'd like. Water weekly if it's dry.

CUTTING TIPS: Cut when the flowers are fully formed and opened, before they start to turn brown. Flowers should last five to ten days in the vase. As I already mentioned, make sure you keep cutting to encourage new growth to form. If they get ahead of you and all the flowers start to look brown and tired, try cutting back all the stems about 3 to 4 inches from the ground and then come back in a week. You'll most likely have all new, fresh-looking flowers!

"Blue Horizon" ageratum

FALL

AMARANTH

(Amaranthus virdis)

PLANT TYPE: Annual from plug

SUGGESTED VARIETIES: "Hot Biscuits," "Hot Chili"

BLOOM TIME: late June – frost

Amaranthus, to me, is the epitome of late-summer flowers. A wild-growing version of these textural flowers can also be seen growing in the hedgerows and roadsides in the fall here in Pennsylvania. These late lovelies add a touch of rustic elegance to any arrangement. They come in upright as well as draping forms if you want to get that "spilling-over" look for a tall arrangement.

GROWING: Plant these in early summer, after the danger of frost is past. Here at Flourish, we also plant plug in mid-to-late summer to make sure we have a fresh stash for late fall. They bloom until frost, and we always end up using most, if not all, of these—especially the rust-colored ones, which go so well with the orange, peach, and deep-red colors that are so great this time of the year. Dig your hole a little larger than the roots, put a pinch of balanced fertilizer in the hole, and cover. Water with fish or seaweed fertilizer. You could put a few more applications of fish or seaweed in the coming weeks, but we find that these plants are very hardy and easy to grow even without much fertilizer. Water every week if it's a dry season. I suggest pinching out the center stem when the plant is about 6 to 8 inches tall, to encourage the side shoots to produce longer, more usable stems.

CUTTING TIPS: Cut when the flowers are fully formed and the color is rich and intense. Flowers should last seven to ten days in the vase.

To dry, cut flowers at their peak color, bunch, and hang them in a cool, dry space. They should be fully dry in two to three weeks.

"Hot Biscuits" and "Hot Chili" amaranth

FALL

COCKSCOMB

(Celosia argentea)

PLANT TYPE: Annual from plug

SUGGESTED VARIETIES: "Flamingo Feather," "Celway Terracotta," "Cramer's Rose," "Crystal Beauty"

BLOOM TIME: July – frost

It's hard to narrow down suggested varieties because there are so many to choose from, and fun new colors keep coming out every year! We love the subtle "Crystal Beauty" and oh-so-popular color "Terracotta," but there are many bright, brilliant colors as well. Some varieties are the "comb" shape (or "brain," if you're being imaginative!), and others are a "plume" shade. It's nice to have some of both, depending on what shape you want for your arrangement. Certain varieties dry better than others. In our experience, it seems to be the darker-colored ones that dry best.

GROWING: Plant in late spring or early summer, after the danger of frost is passed. Dig a hole a bit larger than the roots, put a pinch of balanced fertilizer, and cover. Water with fish or seaweed after planting and give it a few more applications to get it well established. Pinch out the center stem when the plant is 6 to 8 inches tall. This will encourage the side shoots to produce nicer stems for cutting, instead of the plant putting all its energy into that one main stem.

CUTTING TIPS: Cut when the flower is showing vibrant color. Flowers should last five to ten days in a vase. To dry, cut when the flowers are at their peak color. Bunch in groups of five to ten stems and hang upside down for about two weeks in a cool, dry place.

Various "Plume" varieties of celosia

FALL

ORNAMENTAL GRASS

(Poaceae)

PLANT TYPE: Annual or perennial, depending on variety

SUGGESTED VARIETIES: "Feathertop," "Bunny Tails," "Broomcorn Millet," "Frosted Explosion"

BLOOM TIME: Mid-July – frost

Right now, there are so many ornamental grass varieties on the market. People just love them in their landscape, but they also make great additions to floral arrangements, especially in fall. You may already have plenty in your landscape that you can cut, but if you don't, include some in your backyard cutting garden! Some grasses are perennials, and some are annuals—we love them both! Our favorites this year were "Feather Top" and "Bunny Tails" (a perennial and annual, respectively). You could plant whatever variety you choose into either the annual or perennial area of your garden; you will probably just want a single plant if you are planting a perennial and maybe two to four plants if you are planting annuals. Just make sure if you are planting a perennial that you get one that doesn't grow to a large size. Either way, you'll be glad you added these. Because they do so well fresh or dried, they are a great season extender!

GROWING: Dig a hole a little bigger than the roots, cover with soil, and water. There is no need to fertilize. Water weekly if it's dry for the next six to eight weeks. Once it's established, it shouldn't need to be watered again aside from the natural rainfall. At the end of the season, if growing a perennial, cut back all this year's growth to about 3 to 4 inches to the ground.

CUTTING TIPS: Cut when the grasses are fully opened. They last indefinitely in the vase. They naturally dry on the stem if you want to use them in dried projects at the end of the season. We use them all through the winter in arrangements, fresh and dried.

Ornamental grass

FALL

COSMOS

(Cosmos bipinnatus)

PLANT TYPE: Annual from seed

SUGGESTED VARIETIES: "Double Click," "Sensation Mix"

BLOOM TIME: August – frost

These flowers also fit into the "wildflower" category and are beloved by many for their casual but elegant look. They come in colors of pinks and whites and look amazing dangling at the top of a bridal bouquet or simply in a vase filled entirely with cosmos!

GROWING: Grow by direct-seeding into the soil. You can plant these in early summer through July. We prefer to plant them later because we find they do best for us planted in mid-summer. Scatter seed along your row and cover with ¼ inch of soil. Water after planting and then once a week until they start to bloom, if there is not enough rain.

CUTTING TIPS: Cut flowers when the petals are fully opened and the color is fresh and vibrant. They should last four to six days in a vase. Keep deadheading to encourage new blooms to form. We also love to use the greens in arrangements if you have some to spare. Their fresh green color and airy look is perfect as a backdrop to vivacious summer blooms.

"Double Click" cosmos

FALL

SUNFLOWER

(Helianthus annus)

PLANT TYPE: Annual from seed

SUGGESTED VARIETIES: "Teddy Bear," "Italian White"

BLOOM TIME: July – September

Sunflowers are one of those flowers that have a big fan club. There are many varieties to choose from, but since you have only a small space in which to grow these, you will want to choose ones that stay on the small side. Here at Flourish, we love to grow the varieties that have a different color or shape. The "Teddy Bear" variety is fluffy and vibrant, and the "Italian White Night" is as pale as they come (so far) and has an intriguing dark center. If you have not been a big fan of sunflowers, you might want to try one of these new varieties and see what you think!

GROWING: Directly seed sunflowers into prepared soil. Plant at a depth of ½ inch to 1 inch and cover with soil. Water at planting time and then once a week until they are "on their way." Keep watering if it's especially dry. The key to raising sunflowers that don't take over your bouquet is to plant the seeds very close together, about 1 to 2 inches. The closer you plant them to each other, the smaller they will grow. Sometimes we plant them super close so that we have flowers just the right size for a groom's boutonniere!

CUTTING TIPS: Cut when the first petals have just started to lift off the center disk of the flower or when the petals are still at an angle and not flattened out. This will greatly improve bloom time in the vase. They should last seven to ten days in a vase when cut at this stage.

We have not done it yet, but some growers like to dry sunflowers by cutting them at the "fully open stage" and letting them hang upside down in a cool, dry space for about two to three weeks.

"Teddy Bear" sunflowers

FALL

DAHLIA

(Dahlias pinnata)

PLANT TYPE: Tuber

SUGGESTED VARIETIES: "Naomi," "Maarn," "Propero," "Café au Lait," "Crichton Honey," "Cornel Bronze," "Bride to Be"

BLOOM TIME: Mid-July – frost

Dahlias are another flower with too many lovely varieties to narrow it down to just a few. There are so many great colors, sizes, and shapes to choose from. Start by choosing one or two to try, see how you like them, and adjust accordingly the following year.

GROWING: Dahlias are grown from a tuber (similar to a bulb) and need to be planted outside after the danger of frost is passed. Plant at a depth of 4 to 6 inches in well-drained soil amended with compost, and sprinkle some balanced fertilizer in the hole when planting. Do not water at planting time! Dahlia tubers are subject to rot, so just let the spring rains do their job. Once they sprout, start to water about once a week. We like to water with fish or seaweed fertilizer to keep them well fed. When you see the first shoots in a few weeks, put Sluggo or another slug deterrent around the shoots.

Once the plants are 8 to 10 inches tall, pinch out the center stem so that the plant is forced to put energy in the side shoots. You may start to see insect intrusion, especially if you have been growing dahlias for a few years. We like to spray with something organic whenever possible (such as neem oil).

Once the season is over and you have had two hard frosts, cut the plant back. We keep most of our plants in the ground to overwinter. Cover the cut-off stalk with leaves or straw, cover that with black plastic, and then leave them alone until the following spring, when you start to see new growth. You can get a much earlier bloom, and it's a lot less work than digging them up every fall and then planting again in the spring.

CUTTING TIPS: Dahlia plants do well if they are continually cut! Don't be afraid to cut long stems, even if you are cutting other buds. The longer the stem you cut, the longer the stem that will grow back. Deadhead often to encourage the plant to keep producing flowers. Dahlias last about three to five days in the vase, depending on the variety.

Various dahlias

FALL

EUCALYPTUS

(Eucalyptus)

PLANT TYPE: Annual from plug

SUGGESTED VARIETIES: "Baby Blue," "Polanthamos," "Baby Blue Spiral"

BLOOM TIME: Late July – December

Eucalyptus is a wonderful addition to any cut-flower garden. You will love having fresh, fragrant greenery at your disposal as an addition to your arrangements and later in various Christmas décor.

In warmer climates, eucalyptus is known as a tree, but in our 6b zone, this plant grows as an annual. It has been known to overwinter, but I have found this to be unreliable, so we just replant every year to make sure we have a good-quality, steady supply.

GROWING: Plant eucalyptus in mid- to late-spring in well drained soil. Make a hole a little bigger than the roots, put a pinch of balanced fertilizer in the hole, and cover. Water with fish or seaweed fertilizer after planting and then once a week if possible. These plants like water, so make sure they get at least an inch a week.

CUTTING TIPS: This plant is naturally at home in warm climates, and if you cut from the plant too early in the season, the foliage will promptly wilt. The plant must be grown in the heat for a good amount of time (about two to three months) before you can confidently cut. For us, that means we are not cutting our eucalyptus until August. The good thing is that once it's established, it can handle a few light frosts, so you can enjoy harvesting from this plant into late fall and even early winter—just in time for your Christmas projects! Eucalyptus should last at least seven to ten days in a vase.

"Baby Blue" eucalyptus

FALL

ANEMONE

(Anemone)

PLANT TYPE: Perennial

SUGGESTED VARIETIES: “Honorine Jobert,” “Robustissima”

BLOOM TIME: Early September – early October

Fall-blooming anemone are a welcome addition to the cutting garden because they do not bloom until the fall, which means it’s a fresh new flower during a time that many of the summer- and fall-blooming flowers are starting to tire. They look like a delicate wildflower and are gorgeous in bouquets, where they can have some space of their own to shine.

NOTE: This perennial anemone is not to be confused with the spring-blooming anemone, grown from corms. They are also a gorgeous addition to your cutting garden, but I do not cover them here because they are a bit more difficult to grow.

GROWING: Plant this perennial in the fall or spring, making the hole about twice the size of the root ball. Add a little balanced fertilizer, cover with soil, and water well Water about once a week until it is well established, in about two months. At the end of the season, cut back the foliage to about 4 inches above the ground.

CUTTING TIPS: Cut the flowers once they are completely opened. They should last about five to seven days in the vase.

“Roustissima” anemone

FALL

SEDUM

(Hylotelephium)

PLANT TYPE: Perennial

SUGGESTED VARIETY: "Autumn Joy"

BLOOM TIME: Mid-July – mid-October

This understated perennial is another overachiever in the cutting garden. It is drought-tolerant and doesn't require hardly any attention besides planting it and watering for a few weeks to get it going. Then you can essentially forget about it until you need some fun texture in your bouquets from July to October.

GROWING: Plant in the fall or spring in a hole dug about twice the size of the root ball. Cover with soil, then water. Water to get it established, but once it's stabilized, this flower is very independent. In the fall, cut back the foliage to about 4 inches from the ground.

CUTTING TIPS: We love to start cutting from this plant in mid-July, when the flower clusters are still a beautiful bright green. They make such a fun statement as a texture at this stage. We continue to cut them until mid-October, when the color deepens to a burnt red, which looks great in those late fall arrangements! They should last seven to ten days in the vase.

You can also dry sedum. Cut when the clusters have a nice deep color but before they start to brown. Bunch them together and hang upside down in a cool, dry place. They should be completely dry in two weeks.

"Autumn Joy" sedum

WINTER

I married a man whose favorite season is winter, and although I love the growing season very much, I can now say that I love winter too! I love spending the slower season dreaming, planning, and skiing.

Winter is a time of rest for the garden. It's wonderful to be able to cut some winter greens and berries for the holiday season, but other than that, I look forward to winter as a time of repose, education, and looking ahead to the next year.

The cold weather is very conducive to hiding inside with a cup of tea to plan for the next year. Successful gardening has much to do with planning and timing, but, if you are anything like me, you might find that part challenging. There are so many pressing everyday tasks that some of the critical and time-sensitive things get set aside in the fray. Something I've found helpful is to write out my gardening tasks on a calendar specifically for the garden. That way, when I look at my calendar throughout the growing season, I remember critical things like ordering, fertilizing, and other specific tasks. I also use this time to remind myself to do the things that are important to me, like drying flowers, or dividing a certain perennial for a friend. Take the notes from the chart in this book and transfer it to your calendar in the winter months, when you have more time on your hands. You will thank yourself later!

Also, mark on the calendar when to order or shop for your flowers. There's nothing more disappointing to a gardener than to realize that the window for ordering a personal favorite flower has passed. Some seeds and varieties are extremely popular, so if you want to nab that special variety or flower color, make sure to mark down when the best time is to purchase!

As a flower farm, we are typically ordering about nine to twelve months ahead. As a home gardener, you may not need to order that far in advance, but keep in mind that certain websites sell out of popular varieties quickly.

Winter is a great time to read those flower books or other resources that you haven't had time to look at all season. Research information about the things you have struggled with this year, and make notes on your garden calendar on when to do certain tasks that will help you during peak growing season. Get inspired for the year to come. Make lists of what you want to plant. Maybe this year, you want to focus on a certain color palette for all your flowers. The sky is the limit, but you must take time to plan ahead, and winter is the perfect time!

There are still some gorgeous plants to cut in the winter cold.

WINTER

CYPRESS

(Chamaecyparis)

PLANT TYPE: Woodie/tree

SUGGESTED VARIETY: "Thoweil Hinoki Cypress"

BLOOM TIME: Early winter

When planning the cut-flower garden list, I knew I wanted to include some dwarf varieties of greens for Christmas décor. This evergreen fits the bill in every way. It stays compact and has a gorgeous evergreen color, and the evergreens last a long time in arrangements.

GROWING: Plant in spring or fall by placing in a hole twice the size of the root ball. Amend the soil with compost and add fertilizer made specifically for evergreens. Cover with soil and water well. Water once a week until established (half a year or more, depending on how much rainfall you get).

CUTTING TIPS: Allow the plant a year or two before you cut a decent amount from the tree. You want to trim lightly so as not to damage the tree or strip it too much. As it matures, you will be able to snip a bit more for your projects. Greens should last a few weeks after they're cut. You can spray your greens with water to help keep them hydrated.

"Chamaecyparis" cypress

WINTER

JUNIPER

(Juniperus)

PLANT TYPE: Woodie/tree

SUGGESTED VARIETY: "Trautman"

BLOOM TIME: Early winter

I just love any plant that I can cut for greens, but especially plants that also produce berries! This plant is known for its green/blue berries, which are typically ready just in time for Christmas. We love them in wreaths or any seasonal arrangement that needs some texture. The greens themselves are a soft greenish blue.

GROWING: Plant in spring or fall by digging a hole twice the size of the root ball. Amend the soil with compost and add fertilizer made specifically for evergreens. Cover with soil and water well. Water once a week until established (half a year or more, depending on how much rainfall you get).

CUTTING TIPS: Allow the plant a year or two before you cut a decent amount from the tree. You want to trim lightly so as not to damage the tree or strip it too much. As it matures, you will be able to snip a bit more for your projects. If you want to highlight the fruit, just snip away any evergreens that are hiding the berries. Greens should last a few weeks, depending on how warm the environment is. You can spray your greens with water to keep them hydrated.

"Trautman" juniper

WINTER

WINTERBERRY

(Ilex verticillata)

PLANT TYPE: Woodie

SUGGESTED VARIETY: "Red Sprite" (Use "Jim Dandy" for pollination)

BLOOM TIME: Early winter

This is another plant that takes a little extra work, but I really think it's worth it to include in the garden. The gorgeous, red berries just light up any Christmas décor, and with the new dwarf varieties now available, it's even more feasible to include this in a small garden!

GROWING: Plant in spring or fall, digging a hole twice the size of the root ball. Place some fertilizer for acid-loving plants in the hole and cover. Water well at planting and then continue to water once a week until established—about four months, depending on how much rain you've gotten. Fertilize your plants with a fertilizer for acid-loving plants in spring.

Winterberry needs a male pollinator to produce berries. This plant should be placed less than 50 feet from your garden to ensure that cross-pollination can take place.

CUTTING TIPS: I know this is hard to hear, but cut very little, if anything at all, from your winterberries for the first five years. These plants need some time to put out high-quality branches, and if you cut too hard, too soon, you will end up with a plant that isn't able to recover and will no longer produce nice, full stems for you. Once they get some growth, you can start taking longer stems. Remember, some things in life take time. A garden is a good place to remember that not everything is ready in one year or season. Believe me, it will be so rewarding when you can finally make those gorgeous cuts off your very own winterberry bushes.

"Red Sprite" winterberry

WINTER

DUSTY MILLER

(Centaurea cineraria)

PLANT TYPE: Annual

SUGGESTED VARIETY: “Candicans,” “New Look”

BLOOM TIME: June – December

Dusty miller is one of those plants that is an understated botanical superhero. It may not make the cover of a glamorous gardening magazine, but it’s super easy to grow with very few (if any) problems, it’s a beautiful addition to almost any arrangement, and it may be the longest-lasting cuttable plant in your garden. And although this is available to cut for most of the growing year, I listed it here in the winter section because this is my very favorite time of the year to cut and utilize dusty miller. It truly shines in winter arrangements!

GROWING: Buy plugs in late spring, after the frost. Dig a hole twice the size of the roots, place a little granular fertilizer, and cover with soil. Water and fertilize at planting time. However, this plant doesn’t need much (if any) fertilizer to produce in its growing cycle. Keep it watered once or twice a week until it gets established. You can taper off watering it unless you hit a dry spell. You can also pinch off the top few inches to encourage a bushier plant.

CUTTING TIPS: We try to get as long of a stem as possible, so cut close to the ground. Put into water as soon as possible and let rest a couple hours before you design with it. We find that the plant can take several light frosts and may even make it through the winter unscathed, but no guarantees! Just use and enjoy this plant as long as you can.

“Candicans” dusty miller

PART THREE

THE PROJECTS

Now that you have done all the hard work fostering your garden, it's time to enjoy your flowers in some arrangements, bouquets, and designs that make you happy. These can range from super simple to an arbor full of blooms for a special event you're having. I personally love it all; from straightforward crafts to more-complex projects, I thought it would be fun to include directions for arrangements of varying skill levels. Perhaps you are drained from your day and just want to have some color on your bathroom vanity to make you smile, or maybe you're up for a challenge and want to increase your floral design skills. I hope that this section of the book can serve as some inspiration to do it all.

For these designs, I have used flowers that bloom at roughly the same time. If yours don't match up exactly, just get creative and substitute other flowers that you have blooming in the garden. Or in some cases, you may want to go to a neighboring florist or flower farmers who have flowers that can supplement yours.

BELOW: Coordinate colors in your arrangements.

A Note on Vases

Many of the following projects are very simple, but in just the right vase, they will shine! Invest in bud vases that make you smile and a few vases that are taller, exquisite, and perfectly speak to your personal style. I find it helpful to have at least one large, upright vase for a statement piece in an entryway or food table, and one elongated vase for a low but fabulous centerpiece. Look for pieces that are special and make you happy. Anyone can put 10 stems of larkspur, dahlia, or baptisia in a mason jar, and it will look very nice. But placed in an elegant blue-and-white, copper, pewter, or ceramic vase, it becomes a vision.

Think of the spaces around your house where an arrangement would look ideal. On your foyer table, or the kitchen table, a tiny spot in the powder room, on a shelf in your library, or placed next to your bed. Some locations will call for a tall, thin vase, and others, something long and low. Others will have space for only a short, tiny vase with just one flower. Purchase vases with these spots in mind.

Let's get started with spring, my favorite season in the garden!

Floral-Arranging Supplies

Consider designating or creating a place in a garden shed, garage, laundry room, or somewhere else in your home for flower arranging. Ideally it should be close to a water source, a spacious countertop, and a trash can. Having all your flower-arranging supplies together will make your design process much more enjoyable and will prevent you from running around the house, trying to find the supplies you need.

- Floral clippers/snips – your most-often-used tool! Keep this sanitized and sharp so that your cuts are clean and don't tear the stems.
- Flower buckets – to directly place your stems into after cutting.
- Bleach or dish soap – keeping your buckets and vases clean is essential for longer-lasting flowers.
- Vases – invest in some containers that you absolutely love and speak to your style. You'll find that you get your money's worth out of them, and you'll reach for them again and again. Find some that will hold different-sized arrangements as well as some simple but cool bud vases.
- Floral sleeves – great to have on hand for when you want to give a gift of flowers to a friend!
- An array of candles, candleholders, votives, and tea lights – makes a centerpiece more elegant in a flash.
- Flower food – have a stash of this powder at the ready so you don't forget to add it when preparing your arrangement.

- Oasis – for flower arrangements in shallow vases, or when more stability for the flowers is beneficial.
- Long knife – for cutting oasis.
- Straight wire – for making corsages and boutonnieres, etc.
- Spool wire – for making wreaths.
- Wire cutters – for cutting wire (using your flower clippers for this will chew up the metal blades).
- Floral glue – specially made to be safe to use with fresh flowers.
- Floral tape (waxy) – for making corsages and boutonnieres.
- Floral design tape (sticky) – for anchoring oases to vases or making a grid for a large vase opening.
- Ribbon – for tying hand-tied bouquets.
- Wreath bases – for creating wreaths. Wire, straw, and grapevine are all good options!
- Hot-glue gun – for dried flowers or Christmas projects.
- Chicken wire – for arbor décor and such.
- Zip ties – for hanging arbor décor and so on.
- Corsage bases – for making corsages.
- Pins – for boutonnieres and corsages.
- Pine cones – collect them throughout the year to have on hand for Christmas projects!

EARLY SPRING
Easy

HELLEBORE MAGIC

The very first flowers of the new year will be your hellebores. After the absence of flowers for a few months, these flowers are most welcome! A simple vase full of hellebores is truly a sight for sore eyes.

SUPPLIES

Bud vase

Clippers

FLOWER RECIPE

7 stems hellebore

1. Fill vase with water. Take off any leaves that will sit underwater.

1

2. Place the stems in water. Arrange and cut as needed so that some are higher, some lower, for a relaxed, natural look.

3. Take an extra moment to enjoy your very first flowers of the year!

2

3

EARLY SPRING
Advanced

SPRING WRIST CORSAGE

A wrist corsage is easier than you think. It's just several flower heads or pieces glued onto a base in a beautiful array. Once you do a couple of these, you'll be more comfortable doing them for others. Use smaller flowers and bits of flowers to make sure you keep it to a scale that feels right to adorn a wrist. A giant flower like a dahlia just looks out of place! Other flowers/greens in the garden that are great for corsages include lisianthus, celosia, hydrangea, sedum, nigella, yarrow, dusty miller, blue thistle, and small dahlias.

SUPPLIES

Corsage cuff
Floral glue
Clippers
Dried moss

FLOWER RECIPE

1 – 2 stems "Bridal Crown" daffodils
4 stems grape hyacinth
1 stem hyacinth
5 clusters of hellebore greens

1. **Start by glueing a bit of the dried moss onto the cuff.** This gives a little texture and stability to the flowers that will be glued to the base. Hold the moss down for a minute or so, until the glue has dried a bit.

2. **Snip the daffodil heads.** Cut them so that the flower stem has a very small tail or is almost flush with the back of the flower.

3. **Glue the heads onto the base at different angles.** Again, hold the flower heads for a minute or so, until the glue has dried.

4. **Cut the grape hyacinths very short.** Place glue on the stems and place in between the daffodil heads.

5. **Remove individual florets from the hyacinth.** Glue about five of them into your design.

6. **Cut off about three to five sets of hellebore leaves.** Put glue on the end and underneath the leaves, then tuck under the flowers and over the sides of the corsage.

7. **Go over the corsage and dab extra glue underneath the heavier flowers.** This ensures better adhesion.

5

8. **Place on the recipient's wrist and squeeze the ends together slightly.** It should feel snug but comfortable.

6

7

8

MID SPRING

Easy

JUST TULIPS

When you grow something truly unique like double or parrot tulips, they need to show off a little. Tulips also are unique in that they will continue to "grow" and open after they are cut. Their stems elongate and grow toward the sun, and the petals open wide in the warm temperature of the house. You will notice that after a few days, they may look different than they did when you first brought them indoors. The longer stems make them look a little unruly, and the petals will open and eventually drop, but that's the wild beauty of a tulip. Let them do their natural dance on your table, and enjoy how they change from day to day.

SUPPLIES

Vase with approx. 3-inch opening

Clippers

FLOWER RECIPE

12 tulips

1. **Take off any leaves that will sit underwater.** Cut the tulips to about 1 ½ times the vase height.

2. **Place in the vase, turning the vase as you go to create a spiral.** This helps keeps the tulips in place.

3. **Wait a few days.** Your tulips will continue to grow and open in the vase, filling any empty spaces in the arrangement.

MID SPRING
Advanced

LILAC ARRANGEMENT IN GALVANIZED VASE

Years ago, I saw another flower designer do a lilac-centric arrangement in a galvanized vase, and I fell in love with it. Maybe it has something to do with the texture and color of the lilacs paired with the cool, smooth metal of the gray vase. Regardless, this is a great time of year to pull out this rustic but elegant container and showcase the very fleeting yet beautiful lilacs from your cutting garden!

Tip: Lilacs will last longer if you split the stem by cutting up the stem several inches with clippers or smash the bottom few inches of with a hammer. This allows water to more easily be taken up into the stem to the flowers.

SUPPLIES
A 6-inch-wide galvanized vase
Clippers
Hammer (optional)

FLOWER RECIPE
5 stems lilacs
18 stems various tulips
6 stems allium

1. **Fill the vase with water and split the lilac stems with your clippers or smash with a hammer.** Remove any leaves that will sit underwater. Place the higher lilac stems to one side of the vase, the shorter ones to the other side, creating a swooping shape for your design. Allow the natural bend of the stems to help dictate their placement.

2. **Place the allium at different levels throughout the lilacs.**

3. **Place the tulips in the vase.** Some can be higher and some lower, facing different directions. Turn the vase as you continue to add flowers.

3

4. **Adjust as needed.** Tweak and pull up any flowers that have sunken into the arrangement and look lost.

5. **Enjoy.** Relish the scent of lilacs and the joy of fresh, homegrown tulips while you can!

4

5

LATE SPRING

Easy

SPRING BUD VASES

Usually, bud vase arrangements consist of a few different flowers grouped into one vase. What we're doing today is one type of flower per vase in a grouping. This is so simple but gives a more interesting look—different yet pulled together by a little repetition.

SUPPLIES

5 of your favorite bud vases

Table runner

FLOWER RECIPE

8 stems veronica

8 stems yarrow

8 stems bachelor's button

5 stems larkspur

1. **Fill vases with water.** Remove any leaves that will sit underwater.

2. **Group each flower type together.** Sometimes I like to do this before I place them in the vase and then cut the stems before placing them in the water together.

3. **Do two vases of yarrow.** This adds balance to the design.

4. **Place the bud vases on your table with a runner.**

1

2

3

4

LATE SPRING
Advanced

PEONY BRIDAL BOUQUET

There's probably no other flower from the garden that's more popular for weddings than the peony. Their fluffy petals and elegant shape are unmatched by any other flower. And the fact that they are in season for only a few short weeks out of the year makes them even more special. Let's capture them while we can!

SUPPLIES

Clippers

Floral tape or rubber band

1 – 2 yards of satin or silk ribbon

FLOWER RECIPE

9 stems peonies

6 stems Queen Anne's lace

10 stems nigella

6 stems baptisia

11 stems baptisia leaves

1. **Prepare the blooms.** Strip any leaves that will sit under the ribbon and lower.

2. **Organize your workspace.** Place each type of flower in a group on the surface in front of you. Start the bouquet with the largest, most beautiful peony stem. Surround it with two stems of nigella, Queen Anne's lace, and baptisia leaves, turning the bouquet as you add each element.

1

2

3. **Continue to add flowers, one at a time.** Make sure to regularly turn the bouquet to get a round shape. Standing in front of a mirror can allow you to see the bouquet at a different angle. This helps you see if it has a funny shape or if you have a void in your design.

3

4

5

4. **Continue building.** Turning the bouquet, keep adding the flowers a few of each type at a time, until all are incorporated into the bouquet.

5. **When you have all the flowers in your bouquet, cut the stems so they are all the same length.**

6. **Tie the stems together with floral tape or a rubber band.**

6

7. **Tie off the bouquet with the ribbon.** Place the bouquet in vase with a few inches of water until it's time to give it to the bride!

EARLY SUMMER
Easy

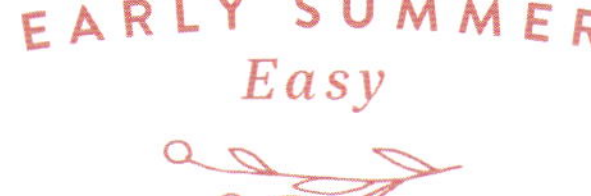

LARKSPUR SOLO

This is another favorite flower of mine, and I love to just enjoy these lovely, long spikes all by themselves. The little buds on the tips of the stems, along with the fullness of the lower florets, make this flower special. If you can, splurge on a tall, beautiful vase of pewter or metal. It will take this very simple arrangement to a whole other level of beauty!

SUPPLIES

Tall vase (about 12 inches) with about a 3-inch-wide mouth

FLOWER RECIPE

15 stems larkspur

1. **Fill the vase with water.** Take off any leaves that will sit underwater.

2. **Place the stems in a crisscross pattern.** This will help them to better support each other in the vase.

3. **Place the higher stems toward the middle.** Then place the other stems around them at different heights to create a natural look.

1

2

3

EARLY SUMMER
Advanced

SUMMER PARTY ARRANGEMENT

This arrangement makes for a great centerpiece! It's a grand and interesting statement, but low enough for conversation to happen across the table. We are using oasis here to make the insertion a little easier, but you could also use a piece of chicken wire, made into a ball and taped onto the vase.

SUPPLIES

A shallow mercury glass compote with about a 6-inch mouth

A small block of oasis or chicken wire

Florist tape (the sticky kind)

FLOWER RECIPE

7 stems sweet William

7 stems scabiosa

6 stems strawflower

6 stems ageratum

3 stems feverfew

3 stems celosia

3 stems amaranthus

10 stems astilbe greens

1 – 2 stems baptisia greens

1. **Drop the oasis into a bucket of water for a few minutes.** Take care not to push the oasis into the water; just let it soak in the water by itself. Tape the oasis (or balled-up chicken wire) onto the compote.

2. **Add the greens.** Place them so that they stretch out to the sides to create the elongated shape.

1

2

3

4

3. **Add flowers.** Place the biggest-headed flowers—the sweet William and straw-flowers—in first. Place them at different levels and angles to create interest.

4. **Add the filler.** Fill in with the smaller flowers: feverfew, celosia, and ageratum.

5

6

5. **Add in the nigella and scabiosa.** Let them dangle and "hang out" of the arrange-ment a bit to create a loose, natural feel.

6. **Add the amaranthus.** This can droop out of the bottom of the compote to add to the loose but classy look of the arrangement.

7. **Add finishing touches.** Fill in any areas where you can see the edge of the vase with any leftover greens or flowers. You want the transition from the vase to flowers to be seamless.

MID SUMMER
Easy

ORANGE, PINK, AND GREEN

This is another super-easy bud vase arrangement, using two classic summer flowers—zinnias and lisianthus—with a fun additional twist, basil!

SUPPLIES

1 bud vase

Clippers

FLOWER RECIPE

2 stems zinnia

1 stem lisianthus

1 stem basil

1. **Fill the vase with water and strip off any leaves that will sit underwater.** Place the basil stem in first, followed by the zinnias. Put the zinnias at two different levels.

2. **Finish by placing the lisianthus in the middle.**

1

2

3. **Find a sweet little spot for this summer delight.**

3

MID SUMMER
Advanced

BOUTONNIERE

Boutonnieres can seem intimidating, but they really do not need to be. Most of the ones that we create have one main flower and a few supporting flowers, with a green leaf to anchor them. Once you can master taping a flower, these will seem like a breeze.

SUPPLIES

Florist straight wire

Floral tape (waxy)

Wire cutters

Clippers

FLOWER RECIPE

1 stem lisianthus

1 stem celosia

1 partial stem eucalyptus

1. **Cut off the top of the lisianthus flower.** Make sure to leave about one to two inches of stem. Place the florist wire through the calyx (the base of the bloom).

2. **Pull the wire down to form a stem.** Cut off at about three fingers' length.

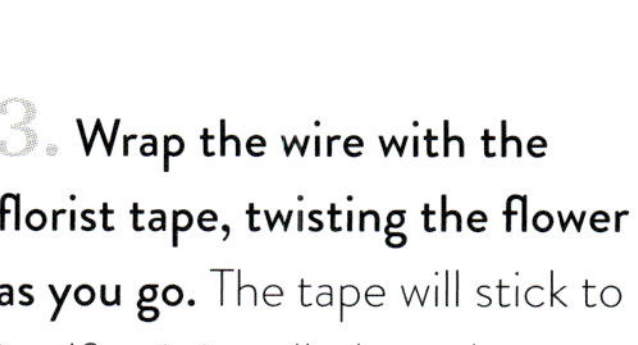

3. **Wrap the wire with the florist tape, twisting the flower as you go.** The tape will stick to itself as it is pulled gently.

4. **Add the supporting flowers.** Incorporate a small stem of celosia and the tip of a eucalyptus stem behind the lisianthus.

5. **Cut them all off at the same length as the wired lisianthus stem.**

6

6. Tape all three together with florist tape.

7

7. Add a pin, and it's ready to go!

LATE SUMMER

Easy

MIXED BUNCH IN A FLORAL SLEEVE

Giving a friend a bunch of your flowers is one of the main reasons we want a cutting garden, right? Let's dress up your gift a tad by adding a flower sleeve. It's such a simple addition, but it looks like it's from an upscale market stand! Floral sleeves are easily found on the internet, and it's great to have them on hand for spontaneous gifts.

SUPPLIES

Floral sleeve

Rubber band

Clippers

FLOWER RECIPE

About 16 stems of any flowers in bloom

For this bouquet we used:

5 stems zinnia

3 stems sunflower

3 stems celosia

3 stems sedum

2 stems cosmos

1. **Strip off any leaves that will sit underwater.** Lay out your flowers in groups.

2. **Start gathering the flowers into your hand, mixing varieties as you go.** Let any delicate flowers hover at the top of the bouquet so you can see them better.

3. **Cut all the stems to one length.** Then, secure them together with a rubber band.

4. **Place the flowers in the sleeve and take to a friend!**

1

2

3

4

LATE SUMMER
Advanced

THE ULTIMATE ARRANGEMENT

This is a fun piece to tackle for those very special occasions! It can be used as a centerpiece (you can see your tablemates and converse underneath its glory), on a food table, and as an entryway piece, or anywhere you need a long, high arrangement. Once you have everything prepped, it's very intuitive to make. Just fill in the oasis and follow the shape of the stand.

SUPPLIES

Tall gold stand

2 blocks of oasis

Floral tape (sticky)

Scissors

Clippers

FLOWER RECIPE

2 large stems eucalyptus

12 stems sedum

12 stems celosia

12 stems dara carota

2 – 4 stems cardinal basil

7 stems dahlias

8 stems lisianthus

2 large stems amaranth

2 stems hydrangea

1. **Drop the oasis in water and let it sit for a few minutes.** Take care not to submerge the oasis in the water. Tape down the oasis with the floral tape.

2. **Cut small stems of the basil.** Intermittently insert them into the sides and top of the oasis. You should be able to get quite a few mini stems from your original stems. Use the dark-red flower heads in addition to the greens.

3. **Place the dahlias in first.** I like to set them at different angles and heights to create interest.

4. **Add the celosia and sedum.**

5. **Add the lisianthus, dara, amaranth, and eucalyptus.** You are on a roll! Let some of the amaranths drape slightly along the sides to create drama. Cut your long stems of eucalyptus into smaller pieces to fill in.

6. **Hydrangeas can be too large for some arrangements, like they are here.** Cut each head into smaller pieces and add Dara.

6

7. **Fill in any empty spaces with the hydrangea pieces.** This type of hydrangea will do excellently out of water, so there's no need to fully insert the small stems into the oasis. Just nestle them down into the arrangement.

7

EARLY FALL

Easy

DAHLIA JOY

After all your love and care to grow dahlias, it's time give them serious admiration. Dahlias shine in any arrangement, but this simple trio begs you to appreciate all the lovely details to be admired in these showcase flowers. I love using three of the same variety, but it would also be fun to mix it up, using different varieties with complementary colors!

SUPPLIES

Ceramic vase with a 1-inch mouth

Clippers

FLOWER RECIPE

3 dahlias

Vase

1. Fill the vase with water.

2. Strip off any leaves that will sit underwater.

3. Place the dahlias at varying heights, facing slightly different directions.

EARLY FALL
Advanced

FALL TABLE ARRANGEMENT

This is another take on the longer, lower centerpiece—this time in a ceramic compote. Something about the naturalistic look of ceramic goes impeccably with the rusty, earthy tones of fall flowers. Fall is a great time to show off the wide variety of textures found in the flowers, grasses, seedpods, and greens of the season. Maybe you'll also want to take a walk down a country lane and cut a few wild elements to add to your arrangement. Either way, this one will be fun to practice your designing skills and experiment with shape, size, and style!

SUPPLIES

Ceramic compote, about 8 inches wide

Oasis (one-third piece)

Floral tape (sticky)

Clippers

FLOWER RECIPE

2 stems sedum

2 stems amaranths

7 medium-sized dahlias

2 – 3 large dahlias

5 – 7 stems eucalyptus

2 – 3 hydrangeas

3 stems rudbeckia

1

1. **Soak the oasis and tape to the vase.**

2. **Place the eucalyptus stems in the oasis.** Longer stems go out to the sides to create a more horizontal shape. Shorter pieces go along the sides and top to keep the shape in check.

2

3. **Place the dahlias in first.** Insert them at different heights and angles to create interest.

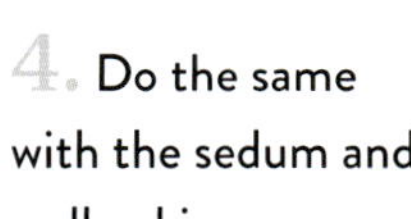

4. **Do the same with the sedum and rudbeckia.**

5. **Cut the hydrangeas into smaller pieces.** (For more on how to do this, see page 171.) Insert them where there are gaps in the arrangement. Then place the amaranthus. This can drape over the sides of the compote to create a romantic, lush look.

6. **Fill in any holes with eucalyptus, keeping the long but not tall shape in mind.** Place in an area where the arrangement has space to stretch out.

6

MID FALL
Easy

DRIED FLOWER WREATH

Although this looks like it took a bit of time, this project is actually very easy, and it's a great way to use some of the dried flowers from your garden. The hoop can be found online or at your local craft store in different sizes. You could substitute other dried flowers from your garden, including yarrow, celosia, sedum, or hydrangea.

SUPPLIES

12-inch gold hoop

Glue gun / glue stick

Dried moss

1 2-foot length of ribbon

FLOWER RECIPE

1 handful dried lavender

6 dried blue thistle

7 dried strawflower heads

1. **Start building.** Glue the moss onto the hoop at the bottom or side, whichever you prefer.

2. **Add the main flowers.** Glue the strawflower heads and blue thistle onto the moss in a natural, random pattern.

3. **Add the supporting flowers.** Cut the lavender to very short stems and glue in between some of the strawflowers and thistle.

4. **Tie the ribbon to the side of the flowers with a simple knot.**

1

2

3

4

MID FALL
Advanced

FALL ARBOR SPRAY

If you've always wanted to dabble in a big floral project, here you go! This project is so exciting to me because all these flowers are sourced from the garden, and it makes such a huge display! A few of the flowers in the recipe are dried. If you find you are low on certain flowers, fresh or dried, just use more of the ones you have a lot of. This would also be gorgeous with spring or summer flowers if you have an abundance!

SUPPLIES

Arbor or structure to hang the sprays

2 rolls of chicken wire, about 18 inches long and 3- to 4-inch diameter

Clippers

6 zip ties

FLOWER RECIPE

25 stems eucalyptus

12 stems celosia

10 stems dara (red Queen Anne's lace)

25 stems dahlias

20 stems lavender greens

10 stems amaranth

10 stems dried nigella pods

10 stems grasses

10 stems hydrangeas

10 stems dried blue thistle

1

1. Start by zip-tying the chicken wire rolls onto the arbor. We typically do the top left corner and the right side, but place them wherever you prefer!

2. Begin inserting the greens into the chicken wire, starting with the eucalyptus. Keep in mind that you are creating the shape of the sprays with your greens. Follow the sides of the arbor as your guide, letting the longest pieces trail out to give a more relaxed feel. Add in the lavender greens.

2

3

3. Tuck in the dahlias and hydrangeas next.

4. Next, put in the celosia and Dara. Make sure not to crowd the flowers you have already placed in the sprays. Some can go deeper into the spray; others can be jutting out from the base. Give each flower space to shine!

5. Place the amaranth so that it drapes down, flowing with your established shape. Then add the blue thistle.

4

5

6. **Add the dried nigella pods and grasses.**

7. **Check the design.** Make sure there are no gaping holes from things that have shifted and look out of place.

LATE FALL / WINTER

Easy

HYDRANGEA TABLESCAPE

Have I mentioned that some of my favorite floral designs are the simplest ones? This one definitely fits that category! It's one of the easiest centerpieces I have ever done, but it always gets lots of comments, and people just think it's amazing. You could redo this design for Christmas with pine cones for the pumpkins and evergreens for the hydrangeas. Or, let your imagination go wild and come up with your own ideas!

SUPPLIES

15 small white pumpkins

A mix of 17 mercury glass votives and glass lanterns, or a variation of what you have on hand

FLOWER RECIPE

16 stems hydrangea heads (can be dried or fresh)

1

2

3

1. **Add light.** Place the votives and lanterns along the center of the table in a long, snaking line. Add the hydrangea heads.

2. **Next, add the pumpkins.**

3. **Light all the remaining candles and enjoy!**

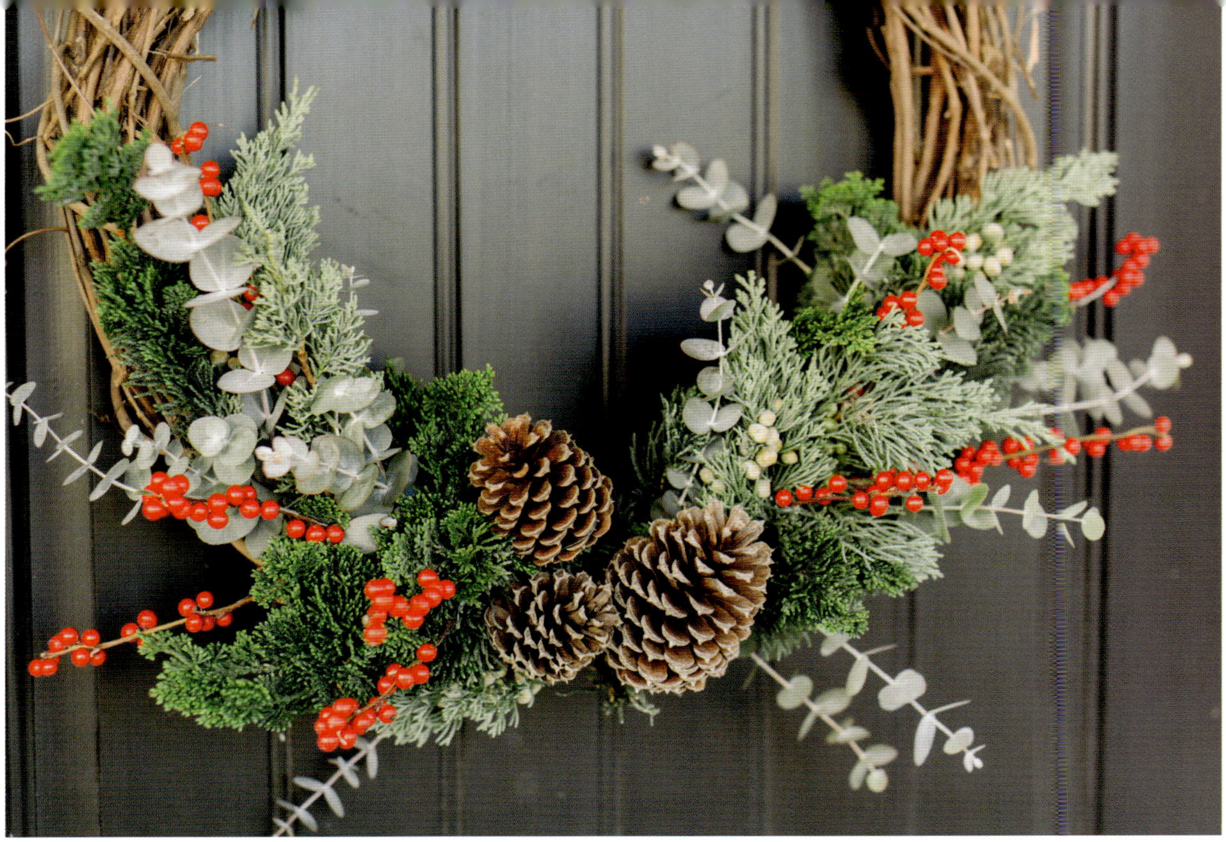

LATE FALL / WINTER
Advanced

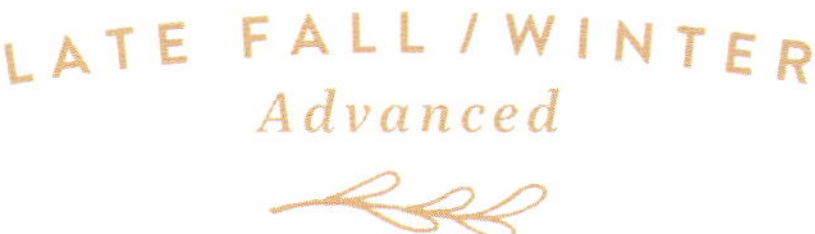

CHRISTMAS WREATH

Greet your guests, neighbors, or passersby with a bit of Christmas cheer by making a winter holiday wreath. All the fresh materials (you guessed it) are from your garden! I loved including a few beautiful evergreens into the garden, especially for the purpose of using them in your Christmas decorations. Plus, a little bit of red winterberry goes a long way to brighten up the greens and make it pop.

SUPPLIES

Glue gun / glue stick
Spool or paddle wire
Wire cutters
12- to 14-inch grape vine wreath base
3 pine cones
Clippers

FLOWER RECIPE

6 stems cypress
5 stems eucalyptus
6 stems juniper
1 stem winterberry

1. **Attach the wire to the wreath base.** Make a little mixed bunch with the greens, and then wire it onto the base by going around the wreath two or three times, wiring the greens at the base of the stems.

2. **Continue making little bunches and lay them on the previous bunch so that the old wire is covered.** Do this until the greens cover about a quarter of the wreath.

3a

3b

3. **Clip the wire and tie off.** Tie the wire on the other side. Do the same thing on this side to create a mirrored second half. The greens should meet at the bottom middle.

4a

4b

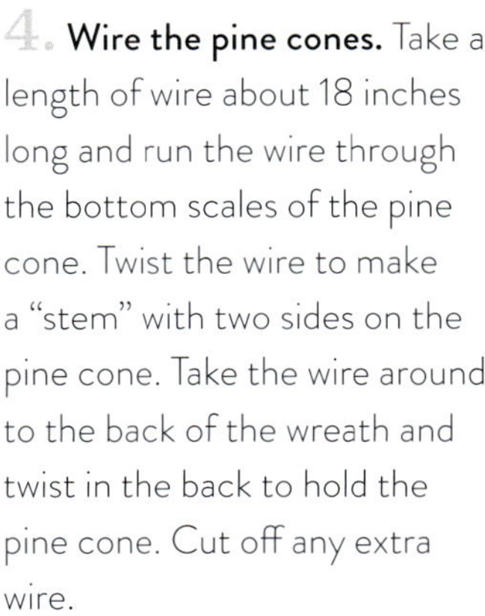
4. **Wire the pine cones.** Take a length of wire about 18 inches long and run the wire through the bottom scales of the pine cone. Twist the wire to make a "stem" with two sides on the pine cone. Take the wire around to the back of the wreath and twist in the back to hold the pine cone. Cut off any extra wire.

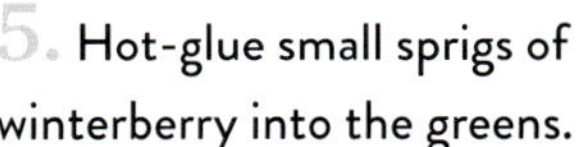
5. **Hot-glue small sprigs of winterberry into the greens.**

5

6. **Display your masterpiece.** Hang on your door to greet your holiday guests!

EARLY WINTER/CHRISTMAS

Easy

WINTER PLACE CARD

This little craft will be a lovely touch to your table, and it will make your guests feel really special! You can do this project a week or so ahead of time. Just keep the finished products in a cool spot so they stay fresh.

SUPPLIES

Glue gun / glue stick

2 4-inch lengths of sticks (can be from a random branch in your yard)

Name tag

Clippers

FLOWER RECIPE

1 tiny sprig of cypress or juniper

1 tiny sprig of winterberry

1. **Begin by gluing the inside of the branches.**

2. **Pinch the name tag in between the sticks.** Make sure it's a bit off-center to allow room for the sprig.

3. **Add the evergreen sprig with some more glue.** Take care to conceal the glue as best you can.

4. **Tuck in the winterberry.** Add more glue if needed.

1

2

3

4

EARLY WINTER/CHRISTMAS
Advanced

HOLIDAY CENTERPIECE WITH TAPERS

This gorgeous textural centerpiece is a great way to adorn your Christmas or winter celebration. It's so satisfying to be gathering all the ingredients for this design from your garden in December. If you keep the oasis watered, this centerpiece should last a couple of weeks.

SUPPLIES

1 block of oasis

Knife

Spool or paddle wire

Wire cutters

Floral tape (sticky)

3 taper candles

12 pine cones

Long silver boat
(or other similarly shaped vase)

Clippers

FLOWER RECIPE

2 stems winterberry

3 – 5 stems dusty miller

10 stems lavender greens

6 stems juniper

6 stems cypress

4 – 6 stems eucalyptus

1. **Cut the oasis into two pieces.** First, cut lengthwise and then cut again to create long, narrow blocks on the boat.

1a

1b

1c

2. **Tape the oasis onto the boat.**

3. **Insert the candles into the oasis.**

4. **Start balancing out your arrangement with the lavender greens.** Follow the shape of the vase as a guide. Longer pieces stretch out to the sides, and shorter ones frame the sides.

5. **Continue with the cypress and juniper.** Make sure you place the juniper stems so that you can see those gorgeous berries!

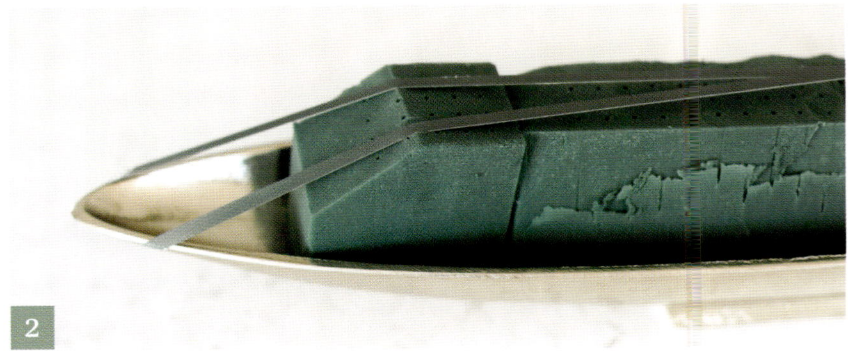

2

3

4

5

6. Add the eucalyptus and dusty miller.

7. Add the winterberries.

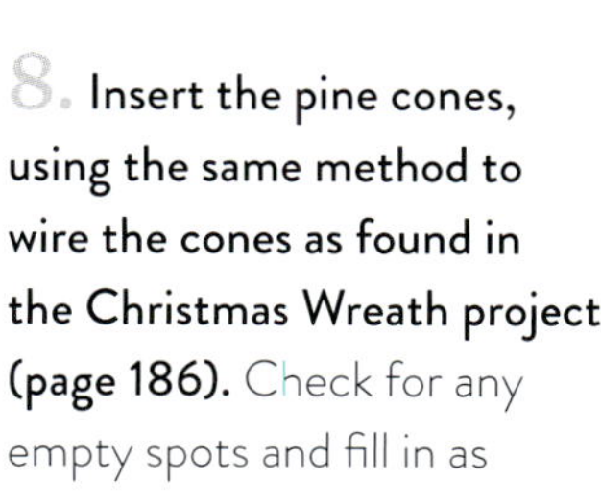

8. Insert the pine cones, using the same method to wire the cones as found in the Christmas Wreath project (page 186). Check for any empty spots and fill in as necessary.

TIME TO REST

It's time to let your garden rest. Time to dream up ways to improve your garden. Time to look at seed and flower catalogs to inspire new ideas. To hold you over, you can also experiment with potted, forced bulbs like hyacinth and amaryllis.

Be assured, spring will come again, and along with it, another year to enjoy your backyard cutting garden and all its incredible bounty.

I have loved going on this journey with you, as you learn what a small cutting garden can produce and what you can create with it. Thanks for coming along with me, and I hope your garden brings you as much joy as mine has brought to me!

INDEX

Note: Page numbers in *italics* indicate specific plant profiles and projects.

GARDEN-PLANNING CHART

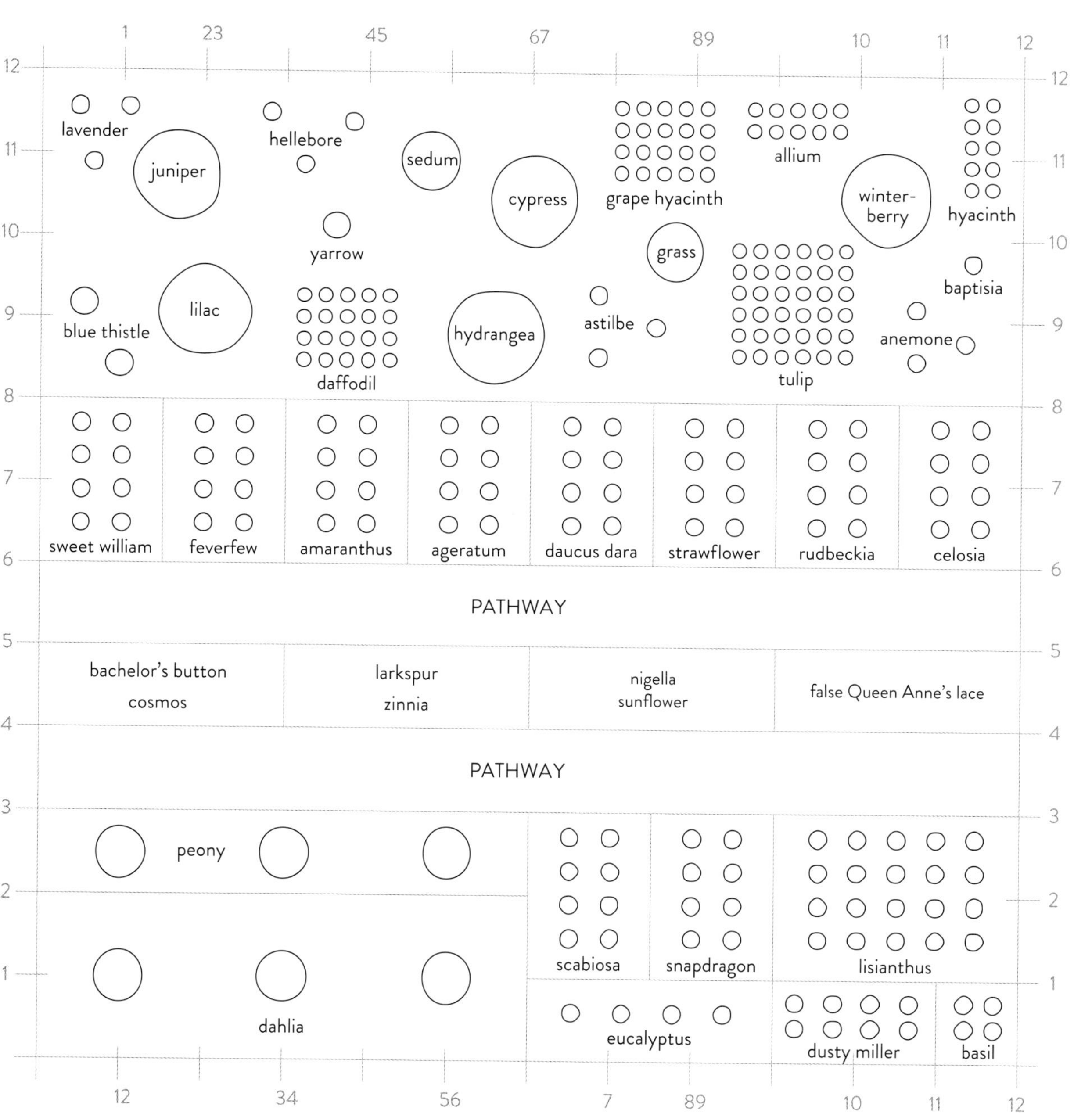

ABOUT THE AUTHOR

I was raised in Montgomery County, Pennsylvania, and grew up among my mother's and grandmother's flower gardens. I always loved being outside in the fresh air but came into my own with gardening after I got married and moved onto my own property.

I started my business in 2001 as a cut-your-own flower garden but soon was asked to make floral arrangements and do weddings for friends, which has steadily led to my increasing the business into florals for all occasions, as well as offering floral classes and events at my location in Lancaster County. I love to encourage, teach, and inspire others to create beauty with flowers.

Together with my loving husband, Bob, I have four adult children, a dog, and a cat.